PHYSICIAN ASSISTANT STUDY BUDDY FOR

DIDACTIC YEAR

Designer: Mesha M. Zeljkovic
Printer: Amazon
ISBN: 9798667959663

DISCLAIMER

Care has been taken to confirm the accuracy of the information present and to describe generally accepted practices. However, the authors, editors, and publisher are not responsible for errors or omissions or any consequences from application of the information in this book and make no warranty, expressed or implied, with respect to the currency, completeness, or accuracy of the contents of the publication. Application of this information in a particular situation remains the professional responsibility of the practitioner; the clinical treatments described and recommended may not be considered absolute and universal recommendations. The authors, editors, and publisher have exerted every effort to ensure that drug selection and dosage outlined in this text are in accordance with the current recommendations and practice at the time of publication. However, given ongoing.research, changes in government regulations, and the constant flow of information relating to drug therapy and drug reactions, the reader is urged to check the package insert for each drug for any change in indications and dosage and added warnings and precautions.

Preface

Get ready to rock your first year of PA school with Study Buddy. Over 3000 fast recall test questions! This book also includes a detailed questionnaire (step by step) on how to obtain patient history, which alone will save you numerous hours prepping for OSCE.

Study Buddy is created because there was no book like this when I went through PA school and I wish I had something like this before or during the school to prepare me better for the first year and save me time while in school. The book is packed with helpful terms, highly tested concepts, buzzwords, fast recall and it will increase your knowledge for the exam.

Study Buddy would be great for anyone thinking about going to PA school to get a sense of what is tested and information learned during the first year. These questions are the once that I studied during my first year and it will help you save time and gain the knowledge to pass your tests during the didactic year of the PA school.

Dedication

To my twins, Mia and Maya,
I dedicate this book to you. You always brighten my day and fill my heart with love. Your two months in NICU though my patience and resilience. Your random hugs and kisses are what drives me to never quit and to be the best father I can be.

To my wife, Megan,
This book and so many other things in my life wouldn't be possible without your never-ending support. I'm forever grateful for your love and support.

When the time comes for EORs and PANCE please check out other PA Study Buddy books.

Table of Contents

Gastrointestinal

Understanding Hep B?	First, look if there is **HBsAg+(hep B surface antigen)** if present than its either acute or chronic. Next look if there is **IgM or IgG**. If **IgM and +HBsAg it's acute** if **+HBsAg and IgG it's chronic**. If it's Anti-HBs + and IgG its recovery from Hep B and finally if it shows only Anti-HBs its immunity from prior vaccination
Increased response to a normally painful stimulus is called what?	Hyperalgesia
The absence of pain in response to normally painful stimuli is called what?	Analgesia
Pain resulting from a stimulus such as light touch that doesn't normally cause pain describes what?	Allodynia
What kind of pain is seen with inner organ damage?	Visceral
Well, localized pain is?	Somatic
What are the 3 regions of visceral pain?	1. Epigastric T4-T8 2. Periumbilical T9-T11, 3. Hypogastric T12-L1
T-4 is at the level of?	Nipples
T-6 is at the level of?	Xiphoid

T-10 is the level of?	Umbilical
T-12 is at the level of?	Pubis
What is the differential diagnosis for RUQ (right upper quadrant) pain?	**Cholecystitis**, Pancreatitis, Pneumonia, Budd-Chiari syndrome
LLQ pain differential diagnosis?	Spleen issues, gastric ulcer, Pancreatitis, **Diverticulitis**
Umbilical region pain differential diagnosis?	**Early appendicitis**, Gastroenteritis, Bowel obstruction, Ruptured aortic aneurysm
Inpatient with acute diverticulitis don't order what test?	Colonoscopy (order CT)
You should consider constipation if the patient reports how many bowel movements per week?	<3 bowel movements per week
What is the most common cause of PUD (Peptic ulcer disease)?	H.Pylori
What is the most common cause of acute pancreatitis?	Alcohol and biliary disease
Gastric cancer is most commonly which type of cancer?	Adenocarcinoma
The most common cause of traveler's diarrhea?	ETEC - enterotoxigenic **E. coli**
What Scoring Systems is used for Acute Pancreatitis?	Ranson's criteria

In patients presenting with **epigastric abdominal pain,** you should always consider what?	Always consider **pancreatitis**
"Colicky" abdominal pain in the **elderly**, think?	Ruptured **AAA** until proven otherwise
Which test should you order for suspected cholelithiasis/cystitis?	US **(any pain in RUQ gets the US)**
If a patient is complaining of abdominal pain in RUQ after a fatty meal, think?	Cholecystitis (Fatty meal, forty years old, female usual stem)
Acute pancreatitis is considered when lipase reaches what level?	3x UNL (upper normal level) (Lipase >500 think pancreatitis)
Name three components of Charcot's triad?	Fever, Jaundice and RUQ pain
Charcot's triad is seen in pt with?	Cholangitis
What's Cullen's sign?	Bluish discoloration of the periumbilical area (acute hemorrhagic **pancreatitis**)
What's Hamman's sign/crunch?	Crunching sound on auscultation of the heart; seen with **Boerhaave's syndrome**, pneumomediastinum, etc.
Pheochromocytoma SYMPTOMS triad?	**P**alpitations, **H**eadache and **E**pisodic diaphoresis (First 3 letters of **PHE**ochromocytoma are P, H, E)
Reynolds' pentad?	Fever, Jaundice, RUQ pain, mental status change and hypotension (think **sepsis** in these patients)

What does Virchow's node indicate?	A metastatic tumor (Gastric cancer primary) to **left supraclavicular node**
What is Boerhaave's syndrome?	Esophageal **perforation**
What is Budd-Chiari syndrome?	**Thrombosis** of hepatic veins
What is the SIRS criteria?	1.Temp >38C <36, 2. WBC >12 <4, 3. HR>90, 4. RR>20 (need 2/4 + infection= Sepsis)
What is the most common cause of infectious diarrhea in children?	Rotavirus
What is the MC medication used to decrease triglycerides?	**Fibric acid** derivatives (Fenofibrate,Gemfibrozil)
What is the most common risk of increased triglycerides?	Acute pancreatitis
What is the most common med used to increase HDL?	Niacin - Vit B3
What is the most common adverse effect of niacin?	Flushing (**Flush that Niacin is how I remembered that**)
What is the most commonplace for AAA?	**Bellow** the renal vessels
Mallory Weiss causes bleeding and Boerhaave's causes what?	Sepsis
A diaphragmatic hernia is common in kids, how would you describe it?	Bowels going up through diaphragm get a **STAT SURGICAL consult**

RUQ and epigastric pain think?	Gallbladder
If the lab results show **ALT > AST** this is indicative of?	Liver issues
Cholecystitis presentation?	RUQ pain and **+Murphy's sign**. Often with N/V.
What is Courvoisier's sign?	Non-tender **palpable gallbladder**
What's dyspepsia?	Early satiation, excessive postprandial fullness, and epigastric pain or burning.
All patients with **dyspepsia** should be **tested for**?	**H.Pylori (Breath urea test)**
What is the most common cause of non GI N/V?	Otitis media
What is jaundice?	Clinical manifestation of **hyperbilirubinemia**, which causes **yellow discoloration of the skin** and sclerae
How do we **diagnose jaundice**?	**Fractionated bilirubin** test
What level of bilirubin will cause jaundice?	**>3**. Bilirubin is a byproduct of heme metabolism
What is the most common cause of **recurrent jaundice**?	Gilbert syndrome (**Gilbert always gets jaundice**)
Abrupt onset of **jaundice with confusion** and petechiae, think?	**Hepatic failure**

Painless jaundice with weight loss, think?	Get a CT abd to r/o **pancreatic cancer**
What is the **most common cause of UGI bleed?**	PUD
History of **cirrhosis and portal hypertension** think?	Esophageal **varices**
History of repeated vomiting or retching think?	Mallory-Weiss tear (**Excessive EtOH drinking leading to retching**)
Side effects of Pepto-Bismol?	**Dark-colored tongue** and stools
With **dysentery diarrhea,** we should expect to see?	**Bloody diarrhea and fever**
Norovirus is MC cause of?	Gastroenteritis- **think cruise ships, hospitals, restaurants.**
Vomiting is a predominant symptom in **which diarrhea?**	Noninvasive diarrhea (No bloody diarrhea) With any diarrhea questions first look if it's bloody or not, if it's not it's noninvasive likely from Norovirus/Rotavirus self-limiting 2-3 days if bloody and fever we got dysentery diarrhea likely shigella or salmonella if it's explosive its shigella if its pets exposure like turtles likely salmonella.
Noninvasive (Enterotoxin) Infectious Diarrhea?	Noninvasive= vomiting, watery, voluminous, no fecal WBCs or blood (**if it has blood that would be dysentery**)
Staphylococcus incubation period?	**W/in 6h.** Food contamination is MCC. Dairy, meat, mayo, and eggs. (**Eating food at the park gathering** in following few hours pt develops

	diarrhea)
How long does staph diarrhea last?	**Self-limiting** 1-2 days. Treatment is supportive
Which bug can cause diarrhea after consuming the fried rice?	Bacillus Cereus **(In B.C. they love fried rice)**
"Rice water stools" severe dehydration, think?	Vibro Cholera **(Rice water vibrates - vibreo)**
Treatment for Vibro Cholera?	Fluid replacement is the mainstay treatment
Which medication is MC cause of C. diff?	Clindamycin **(Clinda Linda makes you poop a lot)**
C diff Signs and symptoms?	Strikingly **increase lymphocytosis (WBC usually >20)**, pseudomembranous colitis, cramps, diarrhea, fever, and tenderness (**Pt will report abx use within last month following with these symptoms**)
C diff treatment?	**Metro**nidazole 1st, Vanco 2nd, or 1st if severe. **Don't give anti-motility drugs in patients with C diff**
How will diarrhea present in **campylobacter enteritis**?	First watery than bloody
Campylobacter enteritis is contracted from?	**Poultry** (turkey) (Eating **turkey at the camp** gives you diarrhea)
Shigella symptoms?	Crampy lower abdominal pain, fever, tenesmus, **explosive watery diarrhea** > mucoid, bloody **(Bloody Shigella)**

Children with shigella can get?	Febrile seizures (**Diarrhea + seizure think shigella**)
Treatment for shigella?	Fluids first if severe TMP/SMT (**Bactrim**)
Pea soup stools, think?	Salmonella (**Salmon pea soup**)
Treatment for salmonella?	Fluids, if severe fluoroquinolones (floxacins) ciprofloxacin (Cipro I relate with Cyprus country, In **Cyprus, they love Salmon pea soup**)
MC cause of gastritis?	H.Pylori
Which test do we order to diagnose gastritis?	Endoscopy is a GOLD STANDARD
How do we treat gastritis/h. pylori?	**CAP** for H pylori-positive (**C**larithromycin, **A**moxicillin, and **P**PI like Omeprazole, think **CAP** for treatment)
"Backpackers diarrhea" think?	Giardia Lamblia (**Drinking water from the streams**)
Giardia Lamblia treatment?	Metronidazole (Flagyl)(**Backpacking in metro**)
Frothy, greasy diarrhea?	Giardia Lamblia (**Gi that's some greasy diarrhea**)
MC cause of **chronic diarrhea** in patients with AIDS?	**Crypto**sporidium
The first step in treating constipation?	Increase fluids, fiber, and exercise.
What separates UGI from lower GI bleeds?	Ligament of treitz
Esophageal Stricture treatment?	**Dilation** of stricture combined with acid-suppressive therapy (PPI or H2)
Dysphagia (difficulty swallowing) to solids	Esophageal strictures

that is only gradually progressive is suggestive of?	
Diagnosing of eso. Strictures can be made with which tests?	Barium swallow and EGD
What is the most common cause of esophageal cancer worldwide?	SCC (squamous cell carcinoma) upper 1/3 of the esophagus. Risk factors are EtOH and smoking
What is the most common cancer in the lower 2/3 of the esophagus?	Adenocarcinoma
Esophageal cancer symptoms?	Solid food dysphagia and then fluids later on; **weight loss**, Dx with EGD
Barret's esophagus patients should be screened how often?	Every 3-5 years with EGD
What is the most common type of hiatal hernia?	Type 1. Sliding hiatal hernia (**Hiatal hernia loves to slide**)
How would you describe a hiatal hernia?	Herniation of proximal stomach into the thoracic cavity through diaphragmatic esophageal hiatus
Which ulcers are more common duodenal or gastric?	Duodenal ulcers are 4 times more common
Patients with a duodenal ulcer often state?	That their **pain is alleviated by ingesting food** but worsens about two-to-three hours after eating.
How long should the patient be off PPIs before H.pylori testing?	2 weeks

What is the most common cause of intestinal obstruction in infancy?	Pyloric Stenosis
Pyloric Stenosis incidence is seen with the use of which medication?	Erythromycin
Pyloric Stenosis is rare after what age?	6 months
Pyloric Stenosis MC presents during what age?	95% present in 1st 12 weeks of life
Olive size mass in RUQ, think?	Pyloric stenosis
Projectile vomiting in a baby, think?	Pyloric stenosis (vomiting across the room)
Which Hep is the only one that's causing **spiking fevers?**	Hep A
What's the normal level of AST?	10-40U/L
What's the normal level of ALT?	7-56 U/L
IgM in Hep A indicates what?	Active Hep A
Hepatitis C Virus (HCV) transmission?	Parenteral (IVDU) transmission. Increased risk if blood transfusion before 1992.
How is Hep C diagnosed?	HCV-RNA
Surface antigen for Hep B indicates what?	HBsAg indicates active infection
EtOH hepatitis will have what labs showing?	AST>ALT 2:1 ratio (I remember this by 2:1 like 21 years old to drink)

Cholelithiasis (Lithiasis - stones) risk factors are?	**5F** - fat forty female fair fertile
Cholelithiasis symptoms?	RUQ pain abrupt lasts 30 min **started by fatty means.**
Heparin antidote (reversible agent) is?	Protamine sulfate
What is the best medication to lower LDL?	Statins
Best medication to lower triglycerides?	Fibrates
The best test for dx of cholecystitis?	HIDA scan (rarely used)
The initial test for dx of cholecystitis?	US (**Any pain in RUQ best initial test is the US**) if + it will show **thickened gallbladder**
Treatment for cholecystitis?	Surgery
What's a **left shift** that is seen on CBC lab work?	Bands>6%, sags>62% indicates **infection**
Cholecystitis presentation?	The patient will be complaining of right upper quadrant pain, jaundice, fever (Charcot's triad)
What is the most common cause of Cholecystitis?	Choledocholithiasis leading to bacterial infection, E.coli
Signs and symptoms of cholangiocarcinoma include?	Yellowing of your skin and the whites of your eyes (jaundice) **Intensely itchy skin. White-colored stools.** Fatigue. Abdominal pain. Unintended weight loss.
Diagnostic test for Pancreatitis?	CT
Pancreatitis on x-ray will show what?	Sentinel loop, **colon cut off sign**

Amylase and lipase in **chronic** pancreatitis?	Are usually not elevated
The most common type of pancreatic cancer is?	Adenocarcinoma ductal **90% located in the HEAD of the pancreas**
Symptoms of pancreatic cancer?	**Painless jaundice CLASSIC**
Which procedure can be done for cancer in the pancreatic head?	Whipple procedure (**Whip that pancreatic head**)
A hard mass of feces in the intestinal tract is called what?	Fecalith
Appendicitis is most commonly caused by?	Fecalith
What's the Rovsing sign?	RLQ pain with LLQ palpitation (You push down in LLQ and patient reports the pain in RLQ)
Describe the obturator sign?	RLQ pain with internal and external hip rotation while bending the knee
What's the psoas sign?	Indicates irritation to the iliopsoas group of hip flexors in the abdomen, and consequently indicates that the inflamed appendix is retrocaecal
Ulcerative colitis is limited to?	**Colon.** Begins in the rectum and spreads proximally. Surgical cure **+pANCA/-ASCA**
Apple core lesion on x-ray, think?	**Colon cancer**
Rectal tenesmus is a feeling of?	Being unable to completely empty the large bowel of stool, even if there is nothing left to expel
Rectal tenesmus is most commonly seen in which disease?	IBD - inflammatory bowel disease

Most common location of pain in patients with ulcerative colitis (UC)?	LLQ
What's the hallmark of UC?	**Bloody diarrhea is the hallmark**
Yellow plaques on eyelids are called?	Xanthelasma
Hard, yellow masses found on tendons?	Xanthoma
What's mild hypertriglyceridemia?	150 to 499, moderate is 500 to 886
UC is diagnosed with which test?	Colonoscopy
UC barium swallow study will show which sign?	**Stovepipe sign**
What is the most common location for Crohn's?	Terminal ileum (**Terminate the Crohns**)
Where can Crohn's develop?	Any section of the GI tract from mouth to anus
What is the most common location of pain in patients with Crohn's?	RLQ (**UC is LLQ**)
-pANCA/+ASCA	Crohn's (Crohn didn't pass the PANCE)
+pANCA/-ASCA	UC (U see you passed the PANCE, +pANCA)
How do we diagnose Crohn's?	Colonoscopy: **Skip lesions; Cobblestone appearance**
Best medication for maintenance treatment of Crohn's?	Mesalamine

Post-surgical adhesions are the most common cause of?	SBO - **small bowel obstruction**
SBO (small bowel obstruction) presentation?	**Vomiting of partially digested food**, and obstipation. Bowel sounds are high pitched early; later the bowel becomes silent= hypoactive
What is the most common site of **LBO (large bowel obstruction)**?	**Distal to the transverse colon**
SBO x-ray will show?	Air-fluid levels and **multiple dilated loops of bowel**
What is the most common cause of LBO in adults?	**Colorectal cancer.** Pain comes in waves. Chronic constipation
Non-obstructive, severe **colon dilation >6cm +** signs of systemic toxicity, think?	**Toxic Megacolon**
Explain the progression of colorectal cancer?	Adenomatous polyps into malignancy (adenocarcinoma)
Familial Adenomatous Polyposis (FAP)is the mutation of what gene?	APC gene
Risk factors for CRC (colorectal cancer)?	>50 years of age, red meat diet, low fiber intake
LBO x-ray will show?	**"Northern exposure" sign, and the "coffee bean" sign**
LBO diagnostic test?	CT abd/pelvis
What is the most common location for anal fissure?	Posterior midline

What is the treatment for anal abscess?	Incision and drainage followed by WASH
Which antigen will be increased in CRC (colorectal cancer)?	**CEA** - Carcinoembryonic antigen (**CEA like CIA will find crap you might be hiding in your colon**)
Epigastric **abdominal pain that radiates to the back**?	**Acute pancreatitis**
In pancreatitis, which cells, are injured?	Acinar cells
Increase in ALT is suggestive of?	Gallstone pancreatitis
Diagnostic triad for **chronic pancreatitis**?	**Calcifications**, steatorrhea, and DM
Pancreatic cancer marker?	**CA 19-9 (Pancreas 19)**
When should we start screening for CRC?	At age 50 with colonoscopy every 10 years unless 1st-degree relative has dx of CRC (start at 40 for them)
What is the most common cause of inherited CRC?	Lynch syndrome
What is the most common location in diverticulitis?	The sigmoid colon (LLQ)
Diverticulosis vs diverticulitis?	Diverticul**osis is uninflamed** diverticula, diverticul**itis = inflammation**-causing LLQ pain, fever, leukocytosis
What is the most common cause of acute lower GI bleed?	Diverticul**osis (PUD is for upper GI bleed)**
Diverticulosis is?	Uninflamed diverticula (assoc with low fiber diet, constipation, obesity). Usually no sx but mc cause of acute LGIB.

Diverticulitis is?	INFLAMMED diverticula secondary to obstruction/infection(fecalith)
Flatulence, bloating, and belching with LLQ sudden pain?	Diverticul**itis**
Diverticulitis Treatment?	A liquid diet, stool softeners, surgery if perforated, antibiotics (Cipro or Bactrim + metro)
What is the most common virus causing Gastroenteritis?	Rotavirus for kids and Norovirus for adults
What capillary refill is indicative of dehydration?	>3sec
Where does the appendicitis pain first begin?	**Periumbilical** later moves to RLQ
Appendicitis CBC will show?	Leukocytosis
Buzzwords for pyloric stenosis?	**NON-bilious vomiting, projectile vomiting, olive-shaped mass**
Test of choice for pyloric stenosis?	US
Intussusception most commonly occurs where?	**Ileocolic** junction (**ii ileocecal intussusceptions**)
Intussusception buzzword?	**Currant jelly stool, sausage-shaped mass**
Intussusception test of choice?	Barium contrast **enema**
What level of ALT indicates viral hepatitis?	>500
This hepatitis is seen with coinfection with Hep B?	Hep D

Intermittent rectal bleeding is mc with?	Internal hemorrhoids
Are internal hemorrhoids painful?	No, external are painful.
Does Indirect inguinal hernia reach scrotum?	Yes
In the direct Inguinal hernia, the weakness is in?	**Hesselbach's triangle** (degenerative). Does not reach the scrotum. (Direct **H**ustle - Hustle Hesselbach)
Double bubble appearance on x-ray?	Duodenal atresia
Which hernia can appear at birth?	Umbilical
What's hiatal hernia?	Protrusion of the stomach through the diaphragm via the esophageal hiatus
Indirect Hernia passage?	**Triple I** (Internal, inguinal ring, inguinal canal)
Direct Inguinal hernia?	External canal, **Hesselbach triangle**
Hernia below the inguinal ligament?	Femoral hernia
If patient complaints of **N/V with a hernia**, think?	Suspect **strangulation** sent to **surgery ASAP** no other imaging needed.
Passage of intestine through the **external inguinal ring** at the Hesselbach triangle describes which hernia?	**Direct** Inguinal hernia **(Direct external)**
Night blindness can be caused by a deficiency in which vitamin?	Vit A
What's Scurvy?	Vit C deficiency

Diagnostic test for lactose intolerance?	Lactose breath hydrogen test
Meckel's diverticulum test of choice?	**99m tech**netium pertechnetate/Meckel's scan (**99 meck**)
Pinworm parasite is also known as?	Enterobius vermicularis
What is the most common parasitic intestinal infection?	Pinworms
What test is done for the diagnosis of pinworm?	Cellophane tape test
What is the medication used for pinworm treatment?	Albendazole
What is the most common cause of acute fulminant hepatitis?	Tylenol
Which Heps are chronic?	B, C, D
What is the contraindication for receiving the vaccine for Hep B?	Bakers yeast (if you are a baker you shouldn't get a hep b vaccine)
Immunized for HepB?	AntiHBs only
Recovery Hep B?	AntiHBs and IgG
What is the most common cause of chronic pancreatitis in children?	**Cystic fibrosis**, EtOH in adults
A Japanese man has weight loss, anorexia, early satiety, epigastric	Gastric carcinoma (Increase in Japanese man)

abdominal pain, and a palpable left supraclavicular lymph node?	
Most important RF for gastric carcinoma?	H. Pylori
GERD symptoms?	Burning pain in the chest that usually occurs after eating and worsens when lying down. **Sour or bitter taste in the mouth**
Cholangitis imaging?	Start with US best is ERCP
Crohn's complications?	Fe and B12 deficiency
Crohn's x-ray will show?	**String sign**
A fibrous ring located at the LES (lesser esophageal sphincter) causes only large diameter foods to get stuck?	Schatzki ring (**steak got stuck**)
Swollen, varicose veins at the lower end of the esophagus?	Esophageal varices
The gold standard for GERD diagnosis?	24h ambulatory pH monitoring
B1 deficiency?	Thiamine - EtOH, Wernicke
B3 deficiency?	Pellagra (dermatitis, dementia, diarrhea) **(B3-3D)**
B6 deficiency can cause what?	Sideroblastic anemia, peripheral neuropathy
What inhibits the secretion of gastrin?	Somatostatin

What neutralizes acid in the stomach?	Bicarb
If the perforation is suspected use what contrast?	Gastrografin
What is the most common cause of esophagitis?	GERD get endoscopy
LLQ pain complaint you should order what test?	CT with oral and iv contrast
Treatment for GERD?	**1st lifestyle changes**, 2nd H2 blockers if moderate to severe give PPI, refractory Nissen fundoplication
Appendicitis diagnostic test of choice?	Adults get CT, kids US and pregnant pt get MRI.
Achalasia is described as?	**Bird beak** at LES, dysphagia to both solids and liquids
The corkscrew appearance of the esophagus, think?	Esophageal Spasm
What's Murphy's sign?	Acute RUQ pain with inspiration
Watery stools accompanied by a low-grade fever, headache, nausea or vomiting, and achiness is consistent with a?	Viral gastroenteritis (watery stool/N/V/fever)
Diarrhea alternating with constipation?	IBS
Viral gastroenteritis is the most common cause of?	Acute diarrhea
Giardia is treated with?	Metronidazole (greasy metro)

Lactulose prevents absorption of what?	Ammonia
Tenderness in LLQ with fever think?	Diverticulosis
PPI (proton pump inhibitors like Omeprazole) can cause?	Vit b12 deficiency
Associated with binge drinking alcohol and then vomiting?	Mallory-Weiss tear
Mallory-Weiss tear dx?	EGD
Mallory-Weiss tear tx?	Supportive
The most common cause of Melena?	PUD
Melena can be seen with?	Right-sided colorectal cancers
Destruction of the pancreatic beta-cells would result in?	Type 1 DM
In patients with a first-degree relative with colon cancer, a colonoscopy should be performed every?	5 to 10 years beginning at age 40
Severe abdominal pain in an elderly individual accompanied by acute diarrhea suggests the possibility of?	Ischemic colitis
Iron absorption occurs in which part of the intestine?	Duodenum
What is the most common cause of liver	Entamoeba histolytica

abscess?	
Esophageal varices most commonly occur in pt with?	Cirrhosis
Pulsatile abdominal mass, think?	AAA
Elderly male smoker with acute abdominal pain and history of HTN, think?	AAA
AAA classic presentation triad?	Acute abdominal pain, abdominal distension, and hemodynamic instability
Pruritus ani (itchy anus) in school-aged kids should make you think?	Pinworms
KUB x-ray shows thumbprint sign, think?	Intestinal ischemia
Does cholesterol make up gallstones or kidney stones?	Gallstones

Good luck on your test! You have studied hard and I'm sure you will do just fine, remember "Thousand's and thousand's of students done this before you, so can you PERIOD". **PLEASE DO ME A HUGE FAVOR AND LEAVE AN AMAZON COMMENT FOR THE BOOK. THAT HELPS ME A LOT AND LET'S OTHER STUDENTS KNOW IF YOU FOUND THIS BOOK HELPFUL. THANK YOU!!!!!!**

Cardiology

Treatment for **Prinz**metal angina?	**CCB** (Calcium channel blockers) - Nifedipine **(I would always associate Calcium with milk in my head and also, in this case, I would say Prince had a smooth voice like milk, so when the question asks tx for Prinzmetal I would immediately think milk and look for CCBs in the answers, I encourage you to create associations as they stay in our minds longer and allow you to recall info faster, try it)**
4 patient groups, which will benefit from statins?	1.Clinical ASCVD 2.LDL>190 3. Diabetes patients with LDL 70-189 4. LDL 70-189 and 10-year ASCVD risk score >7.5%
What kind of murmur is Aortic Regurgitation?	Diastolic decrescendo **Blowing** at LUSB (**Blowing murmurs think regurgitation** either Aortic or Mitral if heard at LUSB it's Aortic)
Mitral stenosis is what kind of murmur?	Diastolic rumble best heard at the Apex (**RUMBLE think stenosis** either mitral or aortic, next look where is it heard if RUSB it's Aortic)
The most common cause of aortic stenosis in the USA?	**Calcified aortic stenosis** due to aging
Aortic stenosis presentation triad?	**ASH** - Angina, Syncope and heart failure
The most common cause of Mitral Stenosis?	Rheumatic heart disease
A most common complaint in	Dyspnea

Mitral Stenosis?	
Most common problem with prosthetic valves?	Thrombosis
Most common dysrhythmia?	A. Fib
The most common cause of A.Fib?	CAD (coronary artery disease) and HTN
The most commonly used study to diagnose left atria thrombi?	Echo (used for the treatment of A.Fib to determine the next step)
Pain from nose to naval should get which test?	EKG
What is Beck's triad?	JVD decreased or muffled heart sounds and decreased BP
Beck's triad is seen in pt with?	**Cardiac Tamponade**
UA vs NSTEMI when comes to biomarkers?	UA (unstable angina) will have **normal biomarkers**, NSTEMI will have elevated biomarkers like troponin
Stable angina treatment?	Sublingual **nitro**glycerin
Angina is due to?	Fixed atherosclerotic lessons
Coronary ischemia is due to?	The imbalance between the blood supply and oxygen demand.
The worst risk factor for angina is?	DM
The most common risk factor for angina is?	HTN
The patient had a STEMI on EKG the next step in treatment is?	Revascularization via PCI or fibrinolysis if no cath lab in 4 h
What is the most common cause of MI?	Atherosclerosis

MI presentation?	Retrosternal pain >30 min, pain is not relieved by Nitroglycerin or rest
Bradycardia + chest pain may suggest?	**Inferior wall MI**
Inferior wall MI will involve which vessel?	RCA (**INFRA**, INF-Inferior RCA --> INFRA)
Septal/anterior wall indicates which vessel involvement?	LAD (Great LADs step up - anterior)
Lateral wall indicates which vessel involvement?	LCX
What's considered STEMI equivalent?	LBBB (Left bundle branch block)
How often should cardiac markers be run?	3 sets every 8 hours
LBBB EKG?	Left bundle branch block. **Look for M (bunny ears) in V6.**
RBBB EKG?	**M (bunny ears) is V1.** Broad and deep s wave in V6
EKG must be read w/in what time frame?	Within 10 min
Nitroglycerin should be held for pt taking which medication?	PDE-5 **Viagra** taken within the last 2 days
Lateral leads in EKG are?	1, AVL, V5V6
Anterior EKG leads?	V1-V4
Most common ECG findings showing irregular irregular rhythm?	A.Fib (**irregular irregular**)
Most common condition accompanying pericarditis?	Pericardial Effusion
A most commonplace for AAA?	Below the renal vessels

Which criteria are used for acute rheumatic fever?	Jones
Genetic cardiomyopathy caused by mutation of the cardiac sarcomere is called what?	Hypertrophic Cardiomyopathy aka HOCM
HOCM is characterized by?	Left ventricular hypertrophy
Patients with HOCM are at increased risk for what?	Sudden cardiac death (Young athlete drops dead on the field)
DVT test of choice?	Doppler US
How long will it take troponin to return to normal?	7-10 days
When does the troponin peak?	12-24 hours
When does the CK-MB peak?	12-24 hours
When does the CK-MB return to normal?	3-4 days
ST depressions or T wave inversions think?	NSTEMI or UA (To figure out which one is it look at the biomarkers if elevated its NSTEMI)
How would STEMi show on EKG?	ST elevations >1mm in 2 or more contiguous leads
Narrow QRS means?	**Tachycardia (HR>100)**
Widening of the mediastinum on chest x-ray is seen with?	**Aortic dissection**
Aortic dissection presentation?	**Tearing pain/ripping pain radiating to the back** + severe distress and diaphoresis.
Which criteria are used for endocarditis?	Duke (**Duke has great Endo class**)

What is the most common risk factor for CAD (Coronary artery disease)?	Diabetes
What is the most common cause of chest pain that's not cardio-related?	Acid reflux (GERD)
What are the most common radiating sites in patients with MI?	Jaw and left arm
S3 gallop, think?	Dilated left ventricle (**DLV-S3**)
What is the most common cause of pericarditis?	Viral infection
What is the most common cause of pericarditis in the post-MI patient?	Dressler syndrome
Chest pain relieved by **leaning forward**, think?	**Pericarditis**
What is the Variant (**Prinzmetal**) angina?	Coronary **spasm**, transient ST elevations w/o MI.
What is the most common presentation of Prinzmetal angina?	**Early morning chest pain (question may state the use of cocaine as well)**
In the cocaine-induced Mi avoid the use of?	BB (Beta-blockers), **increased risk of vasospasms**
In which patient population is normal to see sinus bradycardia?	Athletes (athletes can slow their heart down)
Treatment for sinus **brady**cardia?	Atropine (At**rop**ine, I think of rope, Brady I think of Tom Brady, the only sure way to stop Tom Brady is to tie him up with rope)
Fever can cause what sinus rhythm?	Sinus tachycardia (In fever your heart beats fast >100)

Monitoring Warfarin?	Prothrombin time (PT)/International Normalizing Ratio (INR).
Monitoring Heparin?	aPTT
INR normal range?	2-3, under 2 minimal bleeding, >3 excessive bleeding. Check q4-6 weeks
Sick sinus syndrome treatment?	Pacemaker (They have sick syndrome bro, give them pacemaker)
Constant **prolonged PRI >0.2 sec** is what?	**First degree** AV block
Treatment for 1st degree AV block?	None needed
2nd degree AV block most commonly occurs where?	Bundle of HIS (that's **HIS** 2nd block)
3rd degree AV block treatment?	Pacemaker
Pericardial effusion is most commonly caused by?	Pericarditis
Electrical alternans is pathognomonic for?	Pericardial effusion (the fluid around the heart alternates EKG waveforms)
SA node rate?	60-100 beats per minute
AV node rate?	40-60 beats per minute
Atrial **Flutter** EKG will show?	**Sawtooth pattern**
What is the most common cause of skipped heartbeats?	PVC (premature ventricular contractions)
The definitive treatment for A. Flutter?	Radiofrequency **ablation**
What's paroxysmal A. fib timeframe?	Self-limiting within 7 days

Metroplol should be used with caution in patients with which airway disease?	Reactive (asthma/copd)
What's the persistent A.Fib timeframe?	A. Fib lasting >7 days and <1 year
Is rate or rhythm preferred as an initial treatment of A.Fib?	Rate
Ablation can cure cardiac issues?	SVT, A. flutter, WPW (wolf Parkinson's white)
Why are NOAC preferred over the warfarin?	No need to check INR
WPW avoid giving which medications?	**ABCD** adenosine, BB, CCB, Digoxin
How do vagal maneuvers affect the heart rate?	Decreases the HR
Describe Pericardial tamponade?	Its fluid in the pericardium that exerts pressure on the heart and hampers its ability to contract normally
Pericardial tamponade CXR (chest x-ray) will show?	(CXR - **bottle-shaped heart**)
ACE inhibitors can cause what besides the cough?	Angioedema (Cough is #1 complaint in the use of ACEi)
What's V. Tach look like on EKG?	3 or more PVCs in a row no p waves seen
How long does V.Tach need to go on to be considered sustained?	30 sec
Treatment for V.Tach?	If **pulseless defibrillation** and if with the pulse synchronized cardioversion
What are the most common adverse effects of Statins?	Liver issues (don't answer rhabdomyolysis)
Erectile dysfunction can occur with which heart medication?	Beta-blockers

WPW (Wolff Parkinson White) EKG will show?	**Delta waves**, short PR interval, and wide QRS
1st line medication for the treatment of WPW?	**Pro**cainamide (**Pro Wolf**)
What's multifocal atrial pacemaker MAT?	HR>100 with 3 different P waves
MAT is classically associated with which lung disease?	COPD
What is the most common cause of V.Tach?	Prolonged QT
What is the most common cause of Torsade's De Pointes?	Hypomagnesemia
Asystole treatment?	CPR should be started at once followed by epinephrine and atropine
T wave inversion in V1V2 leads, think?	Brugada
Brugada is MC in which patient population?	Asian males
What is the most common cause of syncope?	Vasovagal syncope
Kussmaul sign is what?	Increase JVP on inspiration seen in **Constrictive pericarditis** and **restrictive cardiomyopathy**
Which cardiomyopathy has systolic dysfunction?	Dilated (SDD - systolic dilated dysfunction)
Dilated cardiomyopathy CXR will show?	Cardiomegaly
What is the most common cause of restrictive cardiomyopathy?	**Amy**loidosis (**Amy restricts my heart**)
HOCM ECHO will show what?	**Asymmetric wall thickness**

Where is the HOCM best heard?	LLSB (Left lower sternal border)
Will HOCM intensity go up or down with Valsalva?	It will go up (**HOCM Valsalva UP**)
Med treatment for HOCM?	BB (Beta-blockers)
What is the surgical treatment for HOCM?	Myomectomy
Endocarditis in IV drug users is most commonly caused by which bug?	S. Aureus
The most useful test in diagnosing heart failure is?	ECHO
CHF (Congestive heart failure) CXR will show?	**Kerley B lines**, butterfly pattern
What lab can help identify CHF in pt with dyspnea?	BNP
What BNP level is indicative of CHF?	>100
CHF treatment?	Lasix, Morphine, Nitrates, Oxygen, and Position (upright) **(LMNOP FOR CHF)**
What is the most common valve involved in Endocarditis?	Mitral (tricuspid for IVDU)
If the patient presents with **fever + new murmur** think?	**Endocarditis**
Which echo should be done for endocarditis?	TEE **(Endocarditis drinks TEE-tea)**
When is the blood culture done for endocarditis?	Get 3 sets at least 1 hour apart, before ABX are given
Vasodilators do what?	The decrease in HR and BP. Prevention of heart attack, stroke, and aneurysms.

Aortic stenosis is best heard at which location?	RUSB (right upper sternal border)
Where does the aortic stenosis murmur radiate?	Carotids
What kind of pulse is seen with Aortic stenosis?	Narrow pulse pressure (Narrow pulse in question about murmurs answer aortic stenosis)
Weak dilated pulse?	Pulsus **Parvus El Tardus** (seen with AS)
Paradoxical **split S2**?	**Aortic Stenosis**
Aortic Stenosis treatment?	Valve replacement
What kind of heart failure is seen with Mitral stenosis?	Right-sided heart failure
The only murmur associated with **hemoptysis (coughing blood)?**	Mitral stenosis (MS)(**Ms. why are you coughing blood**)
Where does the MS murmur radiate to?	Nowhere
The opening snap is associated with which murmur?	**Mitral stenosis (MS said oooo snap)**
Mitral valve treatment?	Repair the valve
Syphilis is associated with which murmur?	AR - Aortic regurgitation
What kind of pulse pressure is seen with AR?	Wide pulse pressure
Patient with **head bobbing** has what murmur?	**AR it's a DeMusset sign (AR you head bobbing)**
A water hammer pulse is seen with what murmur?	AR - Aortic regurgitation

What is the most common cause of mitral regurgitation?	Mitral valve prolapse (MVP)
MR murmur radiates where?	Axilla
MR heart sound?	**Widely** split S2
Mid to late systolic ejection click is seen with which murmur?	Mitral valve prolapse (MVP Click)
MVP (mitral valve prolapse) treatment?	BB (HOCM and MVP both can use BB)
"Pericardial knock" is a sign consistent with?	Constrictive Pericarditis
Treatment for pericardial Tamponade?	Pericardiocentesis
MC presentation of PAD (peripheral artery disease)?	Pain with walking relieved with rest (intermittent claudication)
Patient with PAD will have what kind of cap refill?	Decreased
Treatment for PAD?	Cilostazol
MC location for AAA?	Distal to the renal arteries (L2-L4) >3cm is aneurismal
What reduces the shearing force in AAA?	BB (Esmolol, labetalol)
AAA greater than what size needs a repair?	>5.5 cm
Asymptomatic AAA presentation?	Pulsatile abd mass
MC RF for aortic dissection?	HTN
The initial test for suspected AAA?	US

MC site of aortic dissection?	Ascending near the aortic arch.
Use of what drug can cause aortic dissection?	Cocaine
Aortic dissection presentation?	Ripping tearing chest pain radiating to the back
Difference between pulses in upper extremities is seen with?	Aortic dissection
HTN urgency?	Severe (≥ 180/≥ 120 mmHg) hypertension **without acute end-organ damage**. Use CLONIDINE. reduce MAP by 25% within hours. goal BP <160/100
Hypertensive emergency is what?	An emergency created by excessively high blood pressure, which can lead to serious complications such as stroke or aneurysm. **BP >220/110**
Fixed split S2, think?	Atrial septal defect
MC cause of Atrial septal defect?	Ostium secundum
Atrial septal defect location?	Systolic ejection murmur at the pulmonary area LUSB
MC type of congenital heart disease?	VSD Ventricular Septal Defect
VSD is heard best where?	**LLSB, loud high-pitched harsh, holosystolic** murmur
Increased BP in upper compared to lower extremities?	Coarctation of the aorta
What can happen if clonidine is stopped abruptly?	Rebound HTN

HTCZ side effects?	Hyperglycemia caution with DM and gout
MC side effect of CCB?	Constipation
HCTZ functions where?	Distal dilated tubules
Loop diuretics function where?	Loop of Henly (loop in the loop)
Loop diuretics can cause what kind of toxicity?	Ototoxicity
Which diuretic can cause Gynecomastia?	Spironolactone
Beta-blockers side effects?	Impotence, Fatigue, depression
Coarctation of the aorta is associated with which syndromes?	**Turners** and Shones
Coarctation of the aorta diagnostic test?	Angiogram
Coarctation of the aorta x-ray will show?	**Rib notching, the figure of 3**
Machine-like murmur, think?	Patent Ductus Arteriosus (**PDA**)
Patent Ductus Arteriosus (PDA) diagnostic test?	ECHO
Patent Ductus Arteriosus (PDA) treatment?	IV Indomethacin
MC cyanotic congenital heart disease?	**TOF - Tetralogy of Fallot** (Blue is TOF)
TOF x-ray will show?	Boot-shaped heart (**TOF/tough blue boot**)
Angina CP duration?	Last less than 10-15 minutes

Stable Angina CP can be relieved by?	Relieved with rest or nitroglycerin
The best test for cardiac tamponade?	Echo
MC involved a valve with rheumatic fever?	Mitral
HOCM MC initial complaint?	Dyspnea
HOCM intensity increases with?	Valsalva and standing
HOCM intensity decreases with?	Finger squeeze or squatting
A serious cause of syncope in children?	Congenital long QT syndrome
If you suspect the PE which test should you order?	Spiral CTA
Cardiac tamponade will impair?	Diastolic filling of the heart
Congenital long QT syndrome is what QT interval?	>440 milliseconds
Congenital long QT syndrome treatment?	Beta-blockers
What's orthostatic hypotension?	Drop-in systolic BP by 20 or diastolic BP of at least 10
1st line meds for HTN?	Thiazide diuretics
HTN with A.Fib tx?	BB or CCB
Post MI, HTN med of choice?	BB
HTN and DM first choice med?	ACEi
HTN and Osteoporosis?	Thiazide diuretics

JNC 8 goal BP for pt under the age of 60?	<140/90
JNC 8 goal BP for pt over the age of 60?	<150/90
CCB can cause what side effect?	Leg edema
TX for HTN emergency?	Sodium Nitroprusside
What's HTN urgency?	BP >180/120 with no end-organ damage
HTN urgency tx?	Clonidine
Tx for Malignant HTN?	Hydralazine
Peaked p waves?	Right atrial hypertrophy
What is the biggest worry about the V-Tach?	Can progress to V-fib, life-threatening
MCC of V-Fib?	Ischemic heart disease
In pt with CAD, what is the goal LDL?	<100
Edema could signify?	Right-sided HF
The best initial management of all forms of pulselessness is?	CPR
MC risk factor for (peripheral vascular disease) PVD?	Smoking
PVD presentation?	Diminished or absent pulses, muscular atrophy, decreased hair growth, thick toenails, cool skin
PVD initial test?	ABI normal is 0.9-1.3

Harsh rumble sounds are associate with which murmurs?	AS, MS (MS will rumble your AS)
Blowing sound?	AR, MR (Blow the Roof off, Roof for R in AR and MR)
When is the vena cava filter indicated for the treatment of DVT?	For patients in whom anticoagulation is contraindicated
Radiating chest pain often relieved by sitting up or bending forward and worsened by lying down or breathing in and friction rub?	Pericarditis
Fainting or sudden loss of consciousness caused by lack of blood supply to the cerebrum?	Syncope
Mid to late systolic **ejection click** is seen with which murmur?	Mitral valve prolapse (**MVP Click**)
PVD vs PAD?	PVD is better with exercise
Tearing chest pain radiating to back means?	Thoracic aortic dissection
AAA imaging?	The US, ct screening for man>65 who have smoked. Angiography is gold
Treatment for aortic dissection?	Start a BB like LABETALOL or Esmolol. Esmolol is the first-line treatment for a hypertensive patient with an aortic dissection
What's considered mild HTN?	>140/90
What's considered severe HTN?	>160/110

MC birth defect?	Congenital heart defect
MC innocent murmur in early childhood?	Still's murmur
MC cause of CHF in the first month of life?	Coarctation of aorta
How do you close a patent ductus arteriosus?	Prostaglandin inhibitor (IV indomethacin)
Where is patent ductus arteriosus loudest?	Pulmonic area
What condition has blue baby syndrome?	Tetralogy of Fallot (remember the though blue boots)
Older man + syncope + abd pain?	AAA
Hypovolemic shock is?	Shock resulting from blood or fluid loss
Obstructive shock is?	The shock that occurs when there is a block to blood flow in the heart or great vessels, causing insufficient blood supply to the body's tissues. tamponade, PE
3 drugs that cause myocarditis?	CTP clozapine, thiazide, pcn.
Fever + positive troponin, think?	Myocarditis
MCC of non-traumatic cv arrest?	Opioid OD
Goal HDL?	>60 mg/dL
Statins are used to lower cholesterol in the blood and reduce the risk of?	Atherosclerosis
Statin MOA?	Inhibit HMG-CoA reductase

Ischemic pain doesn't change with?	Breathing or body position and there is no chest wall tenderness
Unstable a fib treatment?	Synchronize cardioversion (if less than 48h) must be in sync w QRS if shocked on the T wave can cause v-fib
Rate control for A.Fib is done with which agents?	BB or CCB
Which anticoags doesn't need to monitor INR?	Dabigatran
SVT EKG findings?	Narrow QRS, no p wave
Blowing murmurs are?	Murmurs that end in letter R (AR, MR)
Rumble murmurs are?	Murmurs that end in letter S (AS, MS)
What can help diff cv vs pulm causes of dyspnea?	Stress testing
Cholesterol screening is recommended in men every?	5 years beginning at age 35 and women every 5 years beginning at age 45
Pericarditis may cause?	Friction rub and pulsus paradoxus. (PPP pulsus paradoxus pericarditis)
Cough and dyspnea on exertion suggest?	Cardiac etiology
Pt that presents with S3, JVD, orthopnea, think?	CHF
JNC 8 BP goals?	Elderly goal <150/90, Diabetic or CKD goal < 140/90
JVP + crackles?	CHF
JVP + normal pulm exam?	Tamponade or constrictive pericarditis

Systolic HF, think?	Down EF, S3, thin walls, dilated LV
Pt with URI now with HF and + trops/CK-MB?	Myocarditis (**cath lab shows nothing**)
MC type of cardiomyopathy?	Dilated 95%
Apical LT vent ballooning, think?	Takotsubo CM (broken heart)
Which valves are semilunar?	The pulmonary valve and aortic valve
Pulm HTN is seen with which murmur?	Mitral Stenosis
Congenital Rubella Syndrome is associated with which murmur?	Pulm Stenosis
Pulm Stenosis tx?	Balloon valvuloplasty (pulm gets a balloon)
What's the Carvallo sign?	Increased murmur intensity with inspiration
Which murmurs are seen with endocarditis?	AR and MR
Pt on Coumadin should avoid?	Cruciferous veggies they are high in Vit K
Anticoags used for tx of DVT during pregnancy?	LMWH
Apical lift and S4 gallop on the exam, think?	HOCM
S3 gallop, JVD, and bilateral ankle pitting edema?	Dilated Cardiomyopathy (DCM)
Dilated Cardiomyopathy CXR will show?	Cardiomegaly and pulmonary congestion
What two murmurs are most associated with atrial fibrillation?	MR and MS (Mr. and Ms. A.Fib)

Early wide bizarre QRS, no p wave seen?	PVC
Drugs that cause AV blocks?	(ABCD) Amiodarone, beta-blockers, calcium channel blockers, digoxin,
PAC vs PJC?	PAC has different p waves and PJC has no p wave
MC location for ASD?	Patent foramen ovale
Coarctation of aorta tx?	Treatment is balloon angioplasty with stent placement or surgical correction. Surgical repair is usually performed between the ages of 2 and 4 years.
Gold standard dx for cardiac tamponade?	ECHO - shows RV collapse in diastole
Atrial fibrillation and mitral stenosis are common causes of?	Thrombus formation
Aortic regurgitation leads to?	Wide pulse pressures and pistol shot pulses
Aortic stenosis causes, which pulses?	Pulsus Parvus and pulsus Tardus
Lithium use during pregnancy can lead to?	Epstein anomaly (tricuspid valve issue)
Don't use Amiodarone in the setting of?	Torsade's de pointes
The bicuspid aortic valve, think?	Coarctation of the aorta
Ostium secundum is seen with?	ASD
Pulmonary embolism EKG?	S1Q3T3

MSK	
ADR's of bisphosphonates?	IV use can cause Jaw osteonecrosis, don't use with GFR<35
Bisphosphonates are used for?	Used for osteoporosis
Important patient instructions for the use of Bisphosphonates?	Stay upright for 30 minutes after taking the meds.
Which medication shouldn't be used in patients with osteoporosis?	Calcitonin increases the risk of cancer
Who should get a DEXA scan?	Men > 70, Woman >65
How do we diagnose Osteoporosis?	DEXA scan focuses on the femoral neck.
Clinical presentation of osteoporosis?	Decreased height, Kyphosis, Fractures with minimal or no trauma, Bone pain, x-ray findings.
Which meds can cause osteoporosis?	Steroids, Lithium, Tamoxifen
T-score for osteopenia?	(-1 to -2.5)
T-score for osteoporosis?	(> -2.5)
What's Z-score for osteoporosis?	The # of standard deviations from the value of ambulatory individuals of same-sex and age as the patient.
Which medication can help build bone?	Forteo (Teriparatide)
MC (most common) fractures seen in Paget's disease?	Vertebral crush fractures

MC complication from DM?	Neuropathy
MC cause of septic arthritis?	S. Aureus
MC location of septic arthritis?	Knee and hip
MC reason for septic arthritis in the SI joint?	IV drug use
MC organism in acute osteomyelitis?	S. Aureus
How do we acquire osteomyelitis?	Bacteria from the blood get in the bone.
Herniated nucleus pulposus presentation?	Pain down the leg
Herniated disk pain presentation?	Radiating below the knee
Which incontinence is seen in cauda equina?	Overflow
Tenderness at midfoot tarsal-MT joints?	Lisfranc, on the x-ray look for a step off
Inversion of the ankle can damage which ligament?	Lateral ligament (ILL inversion lateral ligament)
Jones vs tuberosity avulsion fx?	Jones is 1.5 cm above tubercle. An avulsion is MC. Jones can progress to necrosis
Eversion of the foot can damage which ligament?	Deltoid ligament (DEL Deltoid eversion ligament)
Jammed finger fx is seen in which joint?	PIP
Boxer fx tx?	Ulnar gutter splint
Patients with osteoid osteoma will complain of what?	Severe pain at night (tx with ibuprofen-NSAIDS)
Bilateral burst fx of C1 is called what?	Jefferson's, it's unstable

C2 fx is called what?	Hangman's fx
MC bug associated with osteomyelitis involving puncture wounds of the foot?	Pseudomonas aeruginosa (Runner stepped on the nail)
Radial head subluxation, think?	Nursemaids elbow
What ligament is involved in Nursemaids' elbow?	Annular ligament (Nurse Ann)
Nursemaids elbow treatment?	Reduction
MC age group for slipped Capital Femoral Epiphysis (SCFE)?	7 to 16
How will leg be rotated in SCFE?	Externally rotation
X-ray of SCFE will show?	Ice cream slipping off a cone
X-ray of SCFE will show which displacement?	Posterior and inferior
If the question talks about an obese adolescent with knee pain and limp think?	SCFE
SCFE pt will have what range of motion decreased?	Internal rotation and abduction
SCFE treatment?	ORIF (open reduction internal fixation)
MC cause of chronic knee pain in young active adolescents?	Osgood-Schllaters Disease
Osgood-Schllaters Disease is located where?	Anterior tibial tuberosity
Osgood-Schllaters Disease treatment?	RICE, NSAIDs, quadriceps stretching
MC age group in scoliosis?	8 to 10, MC in girls

Scoliosis is dx once which angle is >10 degrees?	Cobbs angle measured on AP/Lat films
Most sensitive test for scoliosis?	Adams forward bending test
When is the surgical correction needed for scoliosis?	If cobbs angle is >40 degrees
Congenital hip dysplasia is seen with?	Firstborn girls
Which babies should get an ultrasound test for suspected congenital hip dysplasia?	All-female breech babies
Physical exam tests for congenital hip dysplasia?	Barlow and Ortolani
Treatment for congenital hip dysplasia in kids <6 months of age?	Pavlik harness for 6 weeks
Avascular necrosis of proximal femur?	Leg-Calve-Perthes disease
MC fractured bone?	Clavicle (mc middle third)
MC age group for Leg-Calve-Perthes disease?	4 to 10 (SCFE is usually over 10)
MC benign bone tumor in children?	Osteochondroma
Osteochondroma MC presentation?	Painless mass
Osteochondroma MC location?	Metaphyseal region of the long bones
MC location for enchondroma?	Hands
Bone pain w/o constitutional symptoms, think?	Osteosarcoma
MC malignant bone tumor?	Osteosarcoma

Osteosarcoma MC location?	Metaphyseal region of the long bones
Most commonly osteosarcoma METS go where?	Lungs
Osteosarcoma x-ray will show?	Sunray burst
Ewing Sarcoma x-ray will show?	Onion skin
MC Juvenile rheumatoid arthritis?	Pauci-articular
Pauci-articular MC involves which joints?	Large joints
MCC of shoulder pain?	Impingement syndrome (positive Hawkins test)
If weakness is present in shoulder abduction?	Rotator cuff tear should be suspected
This fx is usually seen with ski accidents twisting fall?	Tibial plateau fx (MCC of compartment syndrome)
What's the volar plate fx?	Hyperextension of PIP
Impingement syndrome tx?	PT (Physical therapy)
Fibromyalgia presentation?	Vague Pain "all over", but esp. in neck, shoulders, hands, low back, knees, poor sleep/memory
Fibromyalgia is?	Diffuse pain of 11/18 trigger points for >3m. muscle bx shows MOTH EATEN appearance
Fibromyalgia treatment?	Regular aerobic EXERCISE and Good SLEEP hygiene. Medications reserved for those who fail the above treatment. AVOID OPIOIDS
Acute pseudogout tx?	Intraarticular steroid injection

Polymyalgia Rheumatica presentation?	>50 yrs+proximal muscle pain+ESR>40, treatment low-dose prednisolone.
Anti-Jo-1, anti-SRP, anti-Mi-2 are seen with?	Polymyositis/Dermatomyositis
Polymyositis treatment?	Steroids high dose followed by methotrexate
HLA-B27 think?	Ankylosing spondylitis, reactive arthritis, ulcerative colitis, psoriatic arthritis
Lateral epicondylitis aka tennis elbow is caused by?	Inflammation of the extensor tendons of the forearm
Tennis elbow tx?	Splinting forearm; PT, injections if PT fails, surgery
Pain at the radial aspect of the wrist?	DeQuervain disease (Seen with new mothers lifting the baby all day long)
DeQuervain disease is inflammation of abductor pollicis longus and which another ligament?	Extensor pollicis brevis
PE test for DeQuervain disease?	Finkelstein test
Swelling at the point of the elbow, spongy "bag of fluid" over olecranon?	Olecranon bursitis
Olecranon bursitis tx?	Conservative
MCC of Cauda equina?	Acute disc herniation
Cauda equina finding?	Bladder dysfunction, saddle anesthesia, stool incontinence, no anal wink
MC shoulder dislocation?	Anterior glenohumeral (posterior is seen in seizures)

Best initial test for RA?	RF
Most specific test of RA?	Anti-cyclic citru peptide antibody (ACCPA for RA)
Which anemia is seen in RA?	ACD (anemia of chronic disease)
Before treating patients with methotrexate test them for?	TB
Sjogren is associated with an increased chance of developing?	Non-Hodgkin's lymphoma
Anterior shoulder dislocation imaging test?	Axillary and Y view on plain films. The humeral head will be inferior/anterior to the glenohumeral fossa
Anterior shoulder dislocation tx?	Reduction
Anterior shoulder dislocation can affect which nerve?	Axillary nerve
MCC of a posterior shoulder dislocation?	Seizure and el. Shock
In posterior shoulder dislocation, the arm will be?	Arm ADDucted, internally rotated
A direct blow to an adducted shoulder can cause?	AC joint dislocation
MC type of elbow dislocation?	Posterior (FOOSH with hyperextension)
Elbow dislocation tx?	Emergent reduction, posterior splint @ 90 degrees x 7-10 days; unstable ORIF
Spilled teacup sign-on x-ray, think?	Lunate dislocation
What's Gamekeeper's thumb?	Sprain or tear of the ulnar collateral ligament of the thumb. Instability of the MCP joint.

The best initial test for SLE (LUPUS)?	ANA
SLE tx?	Refer to a rheumatologist for meds hydroxychloroquine. Pt should avoid the sun.
SLE inducing drugs?	Sulfonamides, hydralazine, INH, Procainamide, phenytoin. SHIPP or HIPPS
Scleroderma dx?	Anti centromere ab
Gamekeepers thumb tx?	Thumb Spica and referral to the hand surgeon
MCC of hip dislocation?	Trauma
MC type of hip dislocation?	Posterior
Hip dislocation complications?	Avascular necrosis, sciatic nerve injuries, DVT, bleeding
Hip dislocation presentation?	Leg shortened, internally rotated and adducted
Legg-Calve-Perthes disease dx?	Hip x-rays
Legg-Calve-Perthes disease tx?	Observation
Blades of grass on x-ray?	Paget disease
Which artery can be raptured in Tibio-femoral dislocation?	Popliteal
MC type of ankle dislocation?	Posterior
What's Jones fx?	Transverse fracture through the diaphysis of the 5th metatarsal
Ankle dislocation tx?	Closed reduction + posterior splint
Jones fx tx?	NWB (None weight barring) x 6-8 wks.

Lis-frank dx imaging?	WB AP/Lat of the foot
Hyperuricemia is a hallmark of which disease?	Gout
Gout will have what kind of crystals?	Needle shaped negatively birefringent urate crystals
Gout x-ray will show?	Mouse bite - punched out lesions
Gout tx?	NSAIDs - Indomethacin
MC location for a herniated disk?	L5-S1
Pt with L4 disk issue will experience pain where?	Anterior thigh pain. Loss of knee jerk
Pt with L5 disk issue will experience pain where?	Lateral thigh pain.
Pt with S1 disk issue will experience pain where?	Posterior thigh pain. Loss of ankle jerk
Osteomyelitis MC bug?	S. Aureus
Sickle cell + salmonella?	Osteomyelitis
MC bug in prosthetic joint infections?	Staph epidermis
The best test for Osteomyelitis?	MRI
Osteomyelitis tx?	Surgery
Septic arthritis dx?	Arthrocentesis, WBC>50000, PMN>75%
Myasthenia gravis is associated with?	Thymoma
Foot drop, what nerve is affected?	Common peroneal tx with ankle splint
Reactive arthritis, also check that pt for?	HIV and chlamydia

Can't see, pee or climb a tree, think?	Reactive arthritis
Reactive arthritis tx?	NSAIDs
Test for reactive arthritis?	HLAB27
Med for Sjogren's after conservative therapy failed?	Cevimeline
Shoulder girdle weakness >3 months?	Polymyositis
Fibromyalgia is what?	The chronic condition with widespread aching and pain in the muscles and fibrous soft tissue (above and below the waist
Fibromyalgia ESR and CRP will be?	Normal
Fibromyalgia Tx?	Amitriptyline
Presence of sciatica, a sharp pain that radiates down the back or side of the leg past the knee, is often a sign of?	Disk herniation with nerve root irritation.
The absent patellar reflex is what nerve?	L4 nerve
Positive Birefringement Crystals?	Calcium pyrophosphate crystals --> pseudogout rhomboid
Polyarteritis Nodosa treatment?	Cyclophosphamide, corticosteroids
CREST acronym, think of which disease?	Scleroderma
Osteoporosis most common fracture?	Vertebra > hip
Osteoarthritis (OA) MC presents where?	Weight-bearing joints (knees, hips, spine)

OA big risk factor is?	Obesity
Heberden's node at DIP and Bouchard node at PIP are seen in?	OA
OA x-ray will show?	Osteophyte formation, joint space loss
OA tx?	Tylenol is #1, NSAIDs, Joint injections
Loss of bone density is called?	Osteoporosis
Osteoporosis diagnostic test?	DEXA scan, Osteoporosis is T score<-2.5 where osteopenia is T score of <-1 to -2.5
Primary Osteoporosis is seen in?	Postmenopausal woman
Osteoporosis tx?	Vit D, calcium, and exercise. Bisphosphonates are first-line meds.
A clinical syndrome characterized by chronic pain and tendon thickening?	Overuse syndrome
What's a mallet finger?	Extensor tendon avulsion after a sudden blow to the tip of an extended finger with forced flexion
Mallet finger tx?	Splint the DIP in uninterrupted extension x 6 weeks
What's Boutonniere deformity?	Hyperflexion at the PIP joint with hyperextension at the DIP
What's Gamekeeper's thumb?	Sprain or tear of the ulnar collateral ligament of the thumb. Instability of the MCP joint.
Gamekeepers thumb tx?	Thumb Spica and referral to the hand surgeon

DeQuervain tenosynovitis tx?	Thumb Spica splint x 3 weeks, NSAIDS x 10-14 days
MC location of clavicle fracture?	Middle third
Wrist drop can be caused by injuring which nerve?	Radial nerve
Fracture of which bone can cause wrist drop?	Mid-shaft humerus fracture
Positive empty can test, think?	Rotator cuff tear should be suspected
MC elbow dislocation?	Posterior
Carpal tunnel syndrome involves which nerve?	Median nerve
Snuffbox tenderness is indicative of?	Scaphoid fracture
Pt with lower back pain reports that his pain is better with leaning forward, think?	Spinal stenosis
Elbow x-ray in a child shows a posterior fat pad and sail sign?	Supracondylar fracture
Bamboo spine, think?	Ankylosing spondylitis
In an ACL tear, which tests will be positive?	Lachman's and Anterior drawer
In a meniscal tear which test will be positive?	Apley and McMurry
Thompson test is done to assess?	Achilles tendon tear
While examining the patients' hands you notice Boutonniere and swan neck deformity, this is indicative of?	RA
Positive birefringent RHOMBOID shaped crystals,	Pseudogout

think?	
Malar butterfly rash on the face, think?	Lupus
Anti-jo-1 antibodies are seen with?	Dermatomyositis
NEEDLE-shaped negative birefringent crystals?	Gout
SITS muscles of the rotator cuff?	Supraspinatus, subscapularis, infraspinatus, teres minor
What's a distal radial fracture with dorsal angulation?	Colle's fracture (CD colles dorsal) dinner fork deformity
Deformity over which degree will require a closed reduction surgically in a Boxer fracture?	>40
Gamekeeper's thumb injury will affect which ligament?	Ulnar collateral ligament
Ankylosing spondylitis starts where?	SI joints
MC inflammatory arthritis?	RA
Greenstick fractures greater than what degree need a referral to an orthopedic surgeon?	15 degrees
Patient complain of knee discomfort with their first few steps after rising, think?	Patellofemoral Syndrome
A sugar tong splint is used primarily for?	The distal ulna and radial fractures
Which sling should be used for clavicle fracture?	Figure of 8
Golfer elbow can affect which nerve?	Ulnar
Tx for a scaphoid fracture?	Thumb Spica, ORIF if displacement >1mm

What's a Boxer fracture?	Fracture of the 4th and 5th metacarpal neck (Pt punched a wall)
Tx for kyphosis >60 degrees?	Milwaukee brace
Morton's Neuroma location?	Between the heads of 3-4 metatarsals
Morning stiffness lasting >30 min, think?	RA
Ulnar shaft fracture with radial head dislocation is called what?	Monteggia fracture
Distal radius shaft fracture with distal radioulnar joint disruption is called what?	Galeazzi fracture
Which nerve can be injured in humerus shaft fracture?	Radial nerve
Is anterior or posterior shoulder dislocation more common?	Anterior
Hangman fracture is what?	Fracture of C2 pedicle
Which test is used to diagnose biceps tendonitis during the physical exam?	Yergason's test

Good luck on your test! You have studied hard and I'm sure you will do just fine, remember "Thousand's and thousand's of students done this before you, so can you PERIOD". **PLEASE DO ME A HUGE FAVOR AND LEAVE AN AMAZON COMMENT FOR THE BOOK. THAT HELPS ME A LOT AND LET'S OTHER STUDENTS KNOW IF YOU FOUND THIS BOOK HELPFUL. THANK YOU!!!!!!**

Neurology

Most common (MC) pituitary microadenoma?	Prolactinoma most are nonfunctional
MC type of headache (HA)?	Tension HA
MC causes of bacterial meningitis in neonates?	Group B Strep, E. coli, and Listeria
MC causes of bacterial meningitis in children 1m to 18 years old?	Neisseria meningitis
MC causes of bacterial meningitis in **adults**?	**S. Pneumo**
Bacterial meningitis treatment for neonates?	Ampicillin
Bacterial meningitis treatment for 1m-18y?	Ceftriaxone and Vanco
Bacterial meningitis treatment for adults?	Ceftriaxone + ampicillin + Vanco
What's Kernig's sign?	Inability to straighten a knee with hip flexion (Indicative of meningitis)
What's Brudzinski sign?	Neck flexion produces knee/hip flexion (the sign of meningitis)
What could be the only sign of meningitis in infants?	Fever
Bacterial meningitis CSF will show?	**Increased** WBC, **Increased** Protein and **decreased glucose**
MC type of dementia?	Alzheimer's
Fixed, false beliefs that lack cultural sanctioning?	Delusions
Word salad is?	Lack of connections between words

Extrapyramidal symptoms are?	Akathisia, dystonia, and parkinsonism
Bells palsy is associated with witch HSV?	HSV1
MC cause of encephalitis?	HSV
Under what Glasgow coma scale score should a patient be intubated?	Intubate that patient if GCS <8
MC type of stroke?	Ischemic due to atherosclerosis
MC cause of hemorrhagic stroke?	Berry aneurysm or AV malformation
MCA (middle cerebral artery) stroke, the gaze is pointing in which direction?	Toward the lesion
Neglect is indicative of stroke in which hemisphere?	Right
LE>UE weakness in a stroke patient, this is indicative of which vessel involvement?	ACA
Which vit deficiency can cause seizures?	B6
First-line treatment for status elipticus?	Ativan or Versed
Pregnant with seizure give?	Mg
Which meningitis has a rapid onset?	Acute bacterial <24h fever, HA, stiff neck, confusion, photophobia
Which aphasia is described as an inability to understand speech?	Wernicke's aphasia
When to start abx in meningitis?	W/in 20 min

Signs of meningitis?	High fever, **stiff neck**, drowsiness, and intense headache; may progress to coma and death within hours of onset
CSF Protein in bacterial meningitis?	>200 High protein and WBC, low glucose, >50%PMNs
What do we give first for meningitis?	Give dexamethasone first before abx
Inflammation of the brain is called what?	Encephalitis
Encephalitis symptoms?	Fever, delirium, dementia, seizures, palsies, paralysis **(FEVER+AMS)**
HSV encephalitis treatment?	Requires immediate IV acyclovir
You believe pt is having a stroke, order?	CT without contrast, blood glucose, and oxygen
4T of tetanus?	Trismus- lockjaw, Tetany- muscle spasm, Twitching and tightness
Guillian-Barre Syndrome (GBS) treatment?	Airway if severe, IVIG, plasmaphoresis
GBS: LP will show?	Increased protein (**Guillian only eats protein**) normal WBC
What is a Myasthenia gravis?	An autoimmune neuromuscular disorder characterized by weakness of voluntary muscles **(destruction of ACH receptors)**
Pain is like a band squeezing the head; this describes what type of HA?	Tension headache
Cluster headache treatment?	Sumatriptan +100% oxygen (give meds if O2 doesn't work 100% 6L by NC)
Peripheral vertigo symptoms?	Acute onset dizzy N/V. **Horizontal nystagmus**

Peripheral vertigo test?	Dixhallpike
Headache that is periorbital in location, think?	Cluster headache
Central vertigo is due to?	Lesions
MC type of seizure in infancy?	Febrile
A febrile seizure is what kind of seizure?	Tonic-clonic
Duration of the simple febrile seizures?	<15 min
Febrile seizure treatment?	Lorazepam if the seizure lasts >5 min
Staring spells, think?	Absence seizure (Petit mal)
Encephalopathy management?	Lactulose, Rifaximin/neomycin decrease bacteria production of ammonia in the gut, decrease protein intake. Liver transplant is a definitive treatment
What is a pre-warning sign for the tonic-clonic seizure?	Auras
MC seizure type?	Complex Partial
Tx for absence seizure?	Ethosuximide or Valproic acid
Valproic acid aka?	Depakote
Levetiracetam aka?	Keppra
TIA - MC cause?	Emboli (usually from the heart)
Two types of strokes are?	Ischemic and hemorrhagic

Lacunar Infarct is caused how?	A very small blood vessel of the brain progressively narrows until completely occludes
The lacunar stroke will show what on CT?	Small punched out hypodense area
Tx for ischemic stroke?	IV Thrombotic - Tissue Plasmogen activator (TPA) helps restore cerebral blood flow, needs to be given within 3 hrs of strokes onset, and check contraindications (risk for bleeds/recent surgery)
Symptoms of an ACA (Anterior cerebral artery) infarction include?	**Contralateral lower extremity weakness** and sensory loss with sparing of the upper extremity and face.
Posterior Cerebral Artery (PCA) infarction symptoms?	Visual hallucinations, **contralateral homonymous hemianopsia**, vertigo, nystagmus, diplopia
Carotid endarterectomy is recommended for?	Management of patients with symptomatic carotid artery disease and 70-99% occlusion
Epidural Hematoma MC affects which artery?	**MIDDLE** meningeal artery
How does epidural hematoma look like on a CT?	Suture to suture (**oval shape not crescent**)(**epi is oval**)
Subdural Hematoma MC cause?	Tearing of subdural veins. **Tearing of the bridging veins** in the elderly. This is a **crescent shape bleed**
"Worst HA of my life"?	Subarachnoid hemorrhage caused by rupture of a **berry aneurysm**

MS (multiple sclerosis) will have which CSF findings?	High IgG **oligoclonal bands**
Young woman with vision issues and extremity weakness, think?	Multiple sclerosis MS
Viral meningitis CSF?	**Increased lymphocytes**, normal glucose
Which beta-blocker is used for the treatment of motion tremor (tremor at rest is Parkinson's)?	Use propranolol
Bell's Palsy tx?	Prednisone, Acyclovir
MCC of SAH?	Rupture of berry aneurysm
Multiple sclerosis MRI will show what?	Multiple foci of demyelination in the white matter.
Prophylaxis for cluster HA?	CCB (Calcium channel blockers)
CSF shows increased RBC, think?	Herpes encephalitis. MRI will show temporal lobe edema
CAG repeats are seen with?	Huntington disease
MC brain tumor in kids?	Pilocytic **astrocytoma**
Cause of meningitis in HIV pt?	Cryptococcus neoformans
Triptans are contraindicated in pt with?	HTN and CV disease
Spine shock with neck flexion in MS pt. What's this called?	Lhermitte phenomenon
Which tremor improves with EtOH consumption?	Essential tremor

TIA tx?	ASA+clopidegrel
TIA cause?	Emboli from heart
Hyponatremia can cause?	Cerebral edema (Decreased Na swells the brain)
Hypernatremia can cause?	Brain cell shrinkage. Correct slowly no more than 0.5 to prevent cerebellar edema
MC vasculitis that's affecting mid-large vessels?	Giant cell
Which Steroid do we use for giant cell arthritis?	If vision loss Methylprednisone if no prednisone
Essential tremor improves with?	Improves with alcohol
Essential tremor can be treated with which medication?	Propranolol
How is Huntington's disease diagnosed?	Genetic testing
Anterior cerebral artery stroke?	Contralateral hemiparesis, leg>arm (ACA leg hurts more)
MCA stroke symptoms?	Contralateral paresis (face and arm) Upper>Lower extremities
PCA stroke symptoms?	Contralateral hemianopia with macular sparing, LOC, N/V,
Treatment for tension HA?	NSAIDs
A child with a seizure under the age of 3 months, we should check for?	Meningitis, check with LP
Test for Myasthenia Gravis?	IV edrophonium (Tensilon)

Myasthenia gravis is?	ACh abs muscle weakness that **gets better with rest**, pupils are speared, MC in young woman, HLA-DR3
The neurogenic inflammatory hypothesis is the most accepted theory explaining?	Migraine headache
An acute headache with ataxia, profuse nausea and vomiting is consistent with a?	Cerebral hemorrhage
Cogwheel rigidity, bradykinesia, and tremors?	Parkinson disease
Delirium is referred to as?	An acute state of confusion, which affects memory and cognition. It usually occurs suddenly over hours to days and is associated with a clouding of consciousness and disruption of the sleep cycle.
Progressive memory loss accompanied by loss of instrumental activities of daily living is consistent with a diagnosis of?	Alzheimer disease. These activities routinely include driving and emotional outbursts control. Patients with Alzheimer's also usually will develop social withdrawal. It is the most common cause of dementia
Tau proteins think?	Alzheimer disease. APO-E4 apolipoprotein on chromosome 19 is associated with increased risk for AD
Levodopa is a dopamine precursor that can cross the blood-brain barrier and helps to replenish what?	Dopaminergic loss in the **substantia nigra** typically associated with Parkinson

Kayser-Fleischer rings seen on an eye exam, think?	Wilson's disease (excess copper builds up in the body)
MC brain tumor in adults?	GBM - Glioblastoma multiforme
Pt with Parkinson's will have what kind of tremor?	Pill rolling/resting
What cranial nerve does Bell's palsy affect?	CN VII (Bells go off at 7 o clock)
Treatment of trigeminal neuralgia?	Carbamazepine (Pt with trigeminal neuralgia need some CARBS- Carbamazepine)
Due to the risk of brainstem herniation, a lumbar puncture is contraindicated when?	If Increased intracranial pressure (>20) is suspected.
Patient CT shows a convex, lens-shaped/oval area of hemorrhage in the right parietal region?	Epidural hematoma
Elderly pt should take which vitamin to reduce the risk of falls and fractures?	Vit D
Herpes Zoster Ophthalmicus affects which nerve?	Trigeminal
Herpes Zoster Ophthalmicus Tx?	High dose of Acyclovir w/in 72h
Acute infection of subarachnoid space?	Bacterial meningitis

Concussion and return to sports?	Single concussion: if + LOC or symptoms of concussion lasting more than 15 minutes NOT to return to play sports until asymptomatic for at least one week. Repeat concussions: if associated with either loss of consciousness or symptoms for more than 15 minutes NOT to return to play sports for that season
Bleed in which brain area will increase the risk of seizure?	Temporal area
Jaw deviation towards the side of the lesion indicates the involvement of which cranial nerve?	Mandibular branch of the trigeminal nerve (CN V3)
Tongue deviation towards the side of the lesion?	The hypoglossal nerve (CN XII)
Loss of dopamine-containing neurons located in the substantia nigra and locus coeruleus?	Parkinson disease
MRI shows cerebral atrophy and atrophy of the **caudate nucleus**?	Huntington Disease
First drug approved specifically to treat chorea associated with Huntington disease?	Tetrabenazine
The Budapest consensus criteria are used for?	Complex regional pain syndrome
Narcolepsy treatment?	Modafinil

Treatment for myasthenia gravis?	Cholinesterase inhibitors - **pyrido**stigmine (sounds like a pyramid) gravis like grave think pyramid is a grave)
MC bug in Guillain-Barre syndrome?	Campylobacter jejuni (I meet Guillian at the camp he was eating a lot of proteins)
Huntington disease is associated with which chromosome?	Chromosome 4
Cogwheel rigidity on physical exam, think?	Parkinson disease
Knee jerk reflex is controlled by?	Nerve root L3-L4
The prefrontal cortex is responsible for?	Executive function and emotional regulation
Where is the Wernicke's area located?	Left temporal lobe
What connects the Broca and Wernicke's area?	Arcuate fusciculitis
A dorsal column of the spinal cord is responsible for?	Proprioception and vibration
The spinothalamic tract is responsible for?	Pain and temperature
CN IV lesion/deficit. Pt is tilting their head to the right, where is the lesion?	The lesion is on the left side. They tilt their head to the opposite side
Most common mononeuropathy from the head trauma?	CN IV deficit
Trigeminal neuralgia affects which cranial nerve?	CN V
CN VIII deficits are?	Dizziness, nystagmus and unilateral hearing loss

Loss of gag reflex indicates damage to which CN?	CN IX
Pupillary light reflex tests which cranial nerves?	CN II and III
Pt understands the speech but can't talk this is which aphasia?	Broca's aphasia
What is the name of the inflammatory demyelinating disease of the CNS?	Multiple sclerosis MS
MS destroys the Myelin produced by?	Oligodendrocytes
Where are the MS lesions found?	In the white matter of the brain, spinal cord, and optic nerve
MS is most commonly found in the people that originate from where?	Northern Europe
A young woman in her 20s presents with vision and bladder issues, think?	MS
The most common symptom of MS is?	Fatigue
MC type of MS is?	Relapsing-remitting
If the lumbar puncture shows oligoclonal bands, think?	MS
How do we diagnose MS?	MRI of the brain
Is Parkinson's hyper or hypokinetic?	Hypokinetic
The most common form of involuntary movement?	Tremor
A most common symptom seen in Parkinson's?	Bradykinesia (finger-tapping, micrographic)

Parkinson's symptoms think TRAP?	Tremor, Rigidity, Akinesia/Bradykinesia, and Postural instability
What's hypomimia?	Decreased facial expressions are seen in patients with Parkinson's
What is Chorea?	Involuntary brief irregular movements that flow randomly from one body part to the other
What medication is used to treat Parkinson's?	Levodopa/Carbidopa
Why is Levodopa combined with Carbidopa?	Carbidopa is added to prevent Levodopa breakdown in the periphery so that it can cross the blood-brain barrier and convert to dopamine
Ankle jerk reflex is controlled by which nerve root?	S1 (sacral)
Most common presenting sign of Parkinson's?	Resting (pill-rolling) tremor
Which medication is used for treatment in younger patients with Parkinson to avoid the use of Levodopa right away?	Use of Dopamine agonist such as Bromocriptine
Huntington's disease usually presents at what age?	Between 30 and 50 years old
Patient reports that his tremor goes away after he drinks alcohol, what kinds of tremor do they have?	Essential tremor
A 4-year-old boy has tics in his face and neck and he also shouts obscene words, think?	Tourette syndrome
What is another name for restless leg syndrome?	Willis-Ekbom disease

How do we treat restless leg syndrome?	Pramipexole (Dopamine agonist)
Patients with Guillian Barre will report what kind of weakness?	Ascending weakness and numbness. (It started in my foot and now it's moving up my leg)
What is the role of prednisone in the treatment of Gillian barre?	None, prednisone is contraindicated.
What is an Uhthoffs phenomenon seen in patients with MS?	Their symptoms get worst in the hot weather
What is the initial treatment for MS?	IV Corticosteroids
What kind of taste disturbance is seen with Bell Palsy?	Anterior 2/3 of the tongue
How do we tell if a patient is having stroke vs Bells palsy by looking at their forehead?	Stroke patient will be able to wrinkle both sides while Bell Palsy is unable to wrinkle the affected side (Bell palsy only affects the face and not extremities like the stroke)
Which migraine is classic migraine one with the aura or one without aura?	Classic migraine is with aura
Headache with photophobia that is pulsatile, think?	Migraine headache
What medication can be used as a prophylactic treatment for migraines?	Calcium channel blockers, beta-blockers
Triptans are used for what?	Used to treat symptomatic migraine.
Which syndrome is associated with a cluster headache?	Horner's syndrome
Cerebral cortex atrophy seen on a CT scan is indicative of what?	Alzheimer's

What is the most common risk factor for vascular dementia?	HTN
Which dementia type is associated with visual hallucinations?	Lewy body dementia
If the headache wakes the patient from sleep consider?	Brain tumor as the cause
What kind of tumor is GBM?	Grade IV astrocytoma
Which brain tumor is associated with neurofibromatosis?	Meningiomas
Brain biopsy of a meningioma will show which cells?	Spindle cells
What do we call a transient episode of neurological dysfunction caused by focal brain, spinal cord, or retinal ischemia?	TIA
What are the risk factors for stroke?	HTN, DM, Smoking, OCP use and other heart issues
How do we evaluate the seizure?	EEG
How long is the seizure treated?	Until seizure free for 1-2 years
What is a prewarning for the tonic-clonic seizure?	Auras
MCC of a posterior shoulder dislocation?	Seizure and el. Shock
What is a MOA of Phenytoin?	Inhibits voltage dependent ION channels
Which seizure medication should be used if the patient also has bipolar disorder?	Valproic acid

The use of OCP decreases the concentration of which seizure medication?	Valproic acid
Which seizure medication has **gingival hyperplasia** as a side effect?	Phenytoin
Which seizure medication is most likely to cause Steven Johnson syndrome?	Lamotrigine
Which seizure medication can cause neural tube deficits (Spina bifida)?	Carbamazepine
If a patient is taking Carbamazepine we should monitor them for what?	Bone marrow suppression
For all pregnant patients with seizures, we must add what to their medications?	Folic acid
Basal ganglia regulate what?	Motor output
Brown-Sequard syndrome will present with?	Ipsilateral weakness, contralateral loss of pain and temp, ipsilateral proprioception and vibration loss
Brown-Sequard syndrome is common in patients with which disease?	MS
Pt with lower back pain reports that his pain is better with leaning forward, think?	Spinal stenosis
Which incontinence is seen in Cauda equina?	Overflow
MCC of Cauda equina?	Acute disc herniation

Cauda equina finding?	Bladder dysfunction, saddle anesthesia, stool incontinence, no anal wink
If dizziness only lasts for seconds, think?	BPPV
If dizziness is present for days, think?	Vestibular neuritis
If dizziness only lasts a few minutes, think?	Migraine
If dizziness is present for hours but not days, think?	Meniers
Bilateral bells palsy, think?	Lyme's disease
Which med is neuroprotective in dementia?	Memantine
Ergotamine shouldn't be used in the treatment of?	Pregnant pt with migraines

Good luck on your test! You have studied hard and I'm sure you will do just fine, remember "Thousand's and thousand's of students done this before you, so can you PERIOD". **PLEASE DO ME A HUGE FAVOR AND LEAVE AN AMAZON COMMENT FOR THE BOOK. THAT HELPS ME A LOT AND LET'S OTHER STUDENTS KNOW IF YOU FOUND THIS BOOK HELPFUL. THANK YOU!!!!!!**

Psychology

MC (Most common) anxiety disorder?	Generalized anxiety disorder (GAD)
Length of time needed for symptoms to be present to be diagnosed with GAD?	6 months
1st line meds for GAD?	SSRI
Hypervigilance, intrusive thoughts, nightmares, and flashbacks, think?	PTSD
MC cause of PTSD in females?	Rape
Length of time needed for symptoms to be present to be diagnosed with PTSD?	1 month
MC medication prescribed for nightmares?	Prazosin (Sleep like a **PRO** no more nightmares)
MC age group diagnosed with panic disorder?	The Mid 20s
Short term meds used for the treatment of panic disorder?	Benzos
Acute stress disorder occurs within?	The first 4 weeks after the trauma
First-line treatment for acute stress disorder?	Trauma-focused CBT
MC mental disorder in the USA?	Social anxiety disorder Phobias
1st line med for performance anxiety?	Propranolol (Beta-blocker) (Perform like a **PRO**)
When should the patient with anorexia nervosa be	When the bodyweight is <20% of normal body weight

admitted?	
When should the medication be started in patients with anorexia Nervosa?	Only after the weight is restored
DSM criteria for Bulimia Nervosa?	Binge/purge at least twice a week x3months
Bupropion (Wellbutrin) blocks which receptors?	NE and dopamine reuptake
Which medication can be used for depression and diabetic neuropathy?	Duloxetine (Due effect)
Hypomanic vs manic episode DSM?	Hypomanic is at least 4 days where manic is at least 1 week
Bipolar II is defined as?	One or more depressive episodes and at least one hypomanic episode
Dysthymic disorder is?	Depressed mood for most of the day, most days for 2 years
Schizophrenia negative symptoms are?	Lack of emotional response, flat affect, alogia, apathy, avolition and blunting
Schizophrenia positive symptoms are?	Hallucinations, delusions, ideas of reference, disorganized speech, tangentiality, and incoherent thoughts
Medication used for schizophrenia with anti-suicidal properties?	Clozapine
Clozapine is the most effective anti-psychotic but caries the risk for?	Agranulocytosis
MC used substance by schizophrenics?	Nicotine (reduces the clozapine level)

Which schizophrenic type has the best prognosis?	Best-paranoid, worst-disorganized type
Best medications for schizoaffective disorder?	Haloperidol or Risperidone
Should schizoaffective patients be admitted?	No, if they are not in danger to themselves or others
MC somatoform disorder?	Conversion
What's the conversion disorder?	Voluntary motor or sensory deficits that suggest a neurologic condition but are medically unexplainable usually preceded by physiological distress
Intentionally faking disorder to assume the sick role without the incentive?	Factitious disorder
Intentionally faking or grossly exaggerating sx for an obvious incentive?	Malingering
Imagined or exaggerated defect in physical appearance?	Body dysmorphic disorder
Personality disorders cluster A?	WEIRD - Schizoid, Schizotypal, Paranoid
Loner, detached, flat affect, restricted emotions, generally indifferent to interpersonal relationships outside the immediate family. Little interest in sexual activity?	Schizoid
Does schizoid pt have fixed delusions?	No (that's paranoid schizophrenia)
Theatrical behavior in the patient?	Histrionic

Grandiosity and lack of empathy?	Narcissistic
Treatment of choice for antisocial?	Psychotherapy
Cluster C personality disorders?	Avoidant, Obsessive-compulsive and dependent
These patients have an intense fear of rejection?	Avoidant PD
Are OCPD patients aware of their problem?	No, they are ego-syntonic
What are the different types of ADHD?	Inattentive, hyperactive/impulsive or combined
What kind of intoxication can cause hyperactivity?	Lead exposure
Which SSRI has the longest half-life?	Fluoxetine
Which SSRI have low sexual SE?	Citalopram, Fluvoxamine, Escitalopram
Refusal to maintain minimally normal body weight is called what?	Anorexia Nervosa
Anorexia Nervosa is dx under what BMI?	<17.5
MC type of child maltreatment in the USA?	Neglect
Autism screening tool?	M-CHAT done at 18 months
Teeth pitting or enamel erosion think?	Bulimia Nervosa

Anorexia Nervosa vs Bulimia Nervosa?	Bulimia Nervosa patients have normal weight or can even be overweight
Bulimia Nervosa treatment?	CBT
Which SSRI can reduce the binge-purge cycle?	Fluoxetine
What's Dysthymia?	Depressed mood for at least 2 years
Anxiety treatment?	SSRIs or Buspirone
The strongest predictor for suicide?	Prior attempt
Which patient population has the highest suicide rate?	Elderly Caucasian males
MC preventable cause of intellectual disability?	Fetal Alcohol syndrome
SSRI MOA?	Block reuptake of serotonin
Akathisia is?	Characterized by a subjective desire to be in constant motion followed by an inability to sit or stand still and consequent pacing.
If pt is taking Zoloft (sertraline) they should avoid?	St. John's wort increases serotonin.
Presence of which gene can be seen in patients with ADHD?	Dopamine transport gene
Which symptoms of ADHD are more likely to be lifelong?	Inattentive
What are the environmental factors for ADHD?	Maternal smoking, preterm birth, low birth weight, and lead exposure

How do we treat ADHD?	Treat it with stimulants like Adderall or Ritalin
What is the worry with the use of stimulants?	Risk of abuse and addiction
If the patient with ADHD is at risk for substance abuse treat their ADHD with?	Atomoxetine
Symptoms of ADHD must be present for how long to be diagnostic?	Symptoms must be present for 6 months
If we are trying to diagnose ADHD the patient has to exhibit symptoms in how many settings?	2+ (home and school)
ADHD is an imbalance between which two hormones?	Dopamine and Norepi
Applied Behavior analysis is a gold standard for?	Autism
A young patient is threatening teachers and bullying other students, this is?	Conduct disorder
What is the treatment for conduct disorder?	Family-based therapy
Which SSRI has GI side effects?	Sertraline
Give two examples of SNRIs?	Duloxetine and Venlafaxine
Wellbutrin has what major side effect?	Decreases the seizure threshold
Give two examples of TCA's?	Amitriptyline and Imipramine
Give two examples of MOA's?	Phenelzine and Selegiline

Serotonin Syndrome, think HARMED?	Hyperthermia, Autonomic instability, Rigidity, Myoclonus, Encephalopathy, and Diaphoresis
What is the number 1 step in treating serotonin syndrome?	Stop taking the meds
The sensory perception that is not derived from existing external stimuli describes what?	Hallucinations
The patient is talking and never gets to the point, this describes which thought process?	Tangential
The patient is telling you a long story around the point but he does end up talking about it, this is which thought process?	Circumstantial
How do we differentiate oppositional defiant disorder from conduct disorder?	ODD will not violate other safety like patients with conduct disorder.
A baby is not showing any expressions of joy by 6 months, this is concerning?	Autism
To diagnose delusional disorder the symptoms must be present for how long?	1 month
The delusional disorder will present as?	A husband is accusing the wife of cheating without any evidence. He thinks about it a lot but it's not interfering with his function at work.

What is the schizophreniform disorder timeline?	Symptoms of schizophrenia are present for less than 6 months (Once the symptoms are presents for >6 months that would be schizophrenia)
What type of hallucinations is most common in patients suffering from schizophrenia?	Auditory
Most common risk factor for schizophrenia?	Family history
An MRI of the brain in a schizophrenia patient may show what?	Enlarged ventricles
What is treatment for schizophrenia?	Antipsychotics (Olanzapine, Risperidone)
What is a problem with using Haloperidol (1st gen antipsychotic) for the treatment of schizophrenia?	Increased extrapyramidal symptoms
What are the extrapyramidal symptoms?	Akathisia, Rigidity, Bradykinesia, and tremor
Lip-smacking and rolling of the tongue in patients taking antipsychotics describes what side effect?	Tardive Dyskinesia
Lithium use during pregnancy can lead to?	Epstein anomaly (tricuspid valve issue)
Lithium MOA?	Increases serotonin and Norepi receptor sensitivity
What is the notable side effect of Olanzapine?	It can cause DM

Will prolactin be increased or decreased with the use of Risperidone?	Increased
Fear of a situation where a patient feels they can't escape is called what?	Agoraphobia (treat with SSRI)
Acute stress reaction vs PTSD?	PTSD is diagnosed once the symptoms have been present for over a month, under a month acute stress reaction
To diagnose ADHD symptoms must be present before what age?	Age 7 in two or more settings (home and school)
Obesity is considered once BMI is over what number?	> 30
Which cluster A personality disorder will present with detachment and social isolation?	Schizoid
Which cluster A personality disorder will present with distrust and suspicion?	Paranoid
Which cluster A personality disorder will present with magical thinking?	Schizotypal
Which cluster B personality disorder will present with promiscuous behavior?	Histrionic
Which cluster B personality disorder will present with unstable relationships and possible self-mutilation?	Borderline
Which cluster B personality disorder will present with a grandiose self-view?	Narcissistic

What is non-suicidal injurious behavior?	Self-directed injurious behavior without the intention of dying
What is the leading cause of death in Americans under age 50?	Drug overdose
Opioid reversal?	Naloxone
How do we treat benzo overdose?	Flumazenil
What defines schizophreniform?	Symptoms present for more than 1 month but less than 6 months
What is catatonia?	An abnormality of movement and behavior arising from a severe neurological or psychiatric condition.
What is acute dystonia?	A stuck muscle or set of muscles resulting within hours to days of starting or increasing an antipsychotic.
What is akathisia?	Sense of restlessness. Happens within days to weeks of staring/increasing an antipsychotic
How long does it take for lithium to work?	7-14 days
What pregnancy complications are associated with lithium?	Epstein anomaly associated with 1st-trimester use
MOA of valproate?	Blocks voltage-sensitive sodium channels, increases brain concentrations of GABA

Neural tube defects and decreased IQ, when taken during pregnancy, is seen with the use of which medication?	Valproate
What is psychosis?	Fundamentally losing touch with reality
What is the most difficult part of hypomania to treat?	The severe depression that follows the episodes
Which benzo has been approved for the treatment of alcohol withdrawal specifically?	Chlordiazepoxide (Librium)
What is the timeframe from acute stress disorder?	Greater than 3 days but less than 1 month
Fluoxetine aka?	Prozac
Which SSRI is associated with lots of diarrhea?	Sertraline (Zoloft)
Which SSRI is associated with QT prolongation?	Citalopram
What do SNRIs do?	They block the reuptake of NE and serotonin
Which SNRI can cause HTN?	Venlafaxine
What are the 3 C's of TCA overdose?	Convulsions, Coma and Cardiac
What is serotonin syndrome?	This occurs when you combine drugs that have serotonergic actions. Patients build up too much serotonin in the synapses.

What is discontinuation syndrome?	Occurs with abrupt cessation of antidepressant (flu-like symptoms)
What is Echolalia?	Repeating of another's words or phrases
What is thought broadcasting?	The belief that the patient's thoughts are audible to others.
What are the ideas of reference?	Believe that the patient is getting special messages from otherwise neutral sources like tv, radio, newspaper, movies
What's Anhedonia?	Having no pleasure in doing things

Good luck on your test! You have studied hard and I'm sure you will do just fine, remember "Thousand's and thousand's of students done this before you, so can you PERIOD". **PLEASE DO ME A HUGE FAVOR AND LEAVE AN AMAZON COMMENT FOR THE BOOK. THAT HELPS ME A LOT AND LET'S OTHER STUDENTS KNOW IF YOU FOUND THIS BOOK HELPFUL. THANK YOU!!!!!!**

Dermatology

Small domed papules with the umbilicated center, think?	Molluscum Contagiosum
Molluscum Contagiosum tx?	Self-limiting (it's a pox virus)
Condyloma is what?	Genital warts type 6 and 11
MC type of skin cancer?	Basal Cell Carcinoma
MC presentation of Eczema?	Scratching and pruritus
MC type of Basal Cell Carcinoma?	Nodular
MC type of Melanoma?	Superficial spreading
MC type of Melanoma in Asians and African Americans?	Acral lentiginous (Asian, African Americans - Acral look for letter A in the answer if you can remember the word)
Four Phases of Healing Process are?	Hemostasis, Inflammation, Proliferation, and maturation
With melanoma, presentation think about ABCD?	Asymmetry, Borders irregular, color, diameter
Eczema herpeticum treatment?	IV Acyclovir
What is RED reaction syndrome?	Syndrome of rapid vancomycin infusion, resulting in skin erythema
Open comedones are what?	Blackheads (closed are whiteheads)

Persistent acne and hirsutism are a red flag for what?	Hyperandrogenism (PCOS, tumors)
Inflammation of pilosebaceous units?	Acne vulgaris
The itch that rashes, think?	Atopic Dermatitis
What's the allergic triad?	Eczema, allergic rhinitis, asthma
MC location for eczema in infants?	Face and extensor surfaces
MC location of eczema in adults?	Flexor surfaces
Tapioca pudding vesicles, think?	**Dyshidrotic** dermatitis
Dyshidrotic dermatitis treatment?	Topical steroid ointment, cold compresses
Oval **coin-shaped** weeping patches?	**Nummular** dermatitis
5 Ps of Lichen planus are?	Purple, popular, pruritis, polygonal and planar
Lichen planus **white oral lacy patches**?	**Wickam striae**
Oral Lichen planus increases the risk for?	Oral cancer
Harold patch should make you think?	Pityriasis Rosea
Pityriasis Rosea will have what pattern of distribution?	**Christmas tree** pattern
Pityriasis Rosea lesions description?	Salmon-colored oval/round papules with white circular scaling, very itchy
Pityriasis Rosea treatment?	None needed its self resolving
Darier's sign?	Localized urticaria appearing where the skin is rubbed

Target lesions should make you think of?	Erythema **Multi**forme (multiple targets - multi/target)
Erythema Multiforme lesion description?	Dusty violet/red, purpuric macule/vesicle, or bullae in the center, surrounded by a pale edematous rim and peripheral red halo.
Erythema Multiforme treatment?	Stop the offending drug, antihistamines, skincare
MC meds causing the SJS and TEN?	Sulfa and anticonvulsant drugs
SJS vs TEN percentage of skin involved?	TEN is >30% and SJS is <10% (TEN is 30+)
MC bug causing the Impetigo?	S. Aureus
Impetigo buzzword?	Honey-colored crusted
Impetigo treatment?	Bactroban 2% ointment if extensive Keflex
MC cause of Molluscum Contagiosum?	Viral (poxviridae family)
Molluscum Contagiosum buzzword?	Dome-shaped, flesh-colored, central umbilication
Lice treatment?	Permethrin 1% shampoo, wash clothing and bedding (Lice and scabies should get a **permit** to park it on the skin, Permethrin)
Scabies buzzword?	Linear burrows
Scabies treatment?	Permethrin 5% cream from the neck down wash it off after 8-14hr, repeat in one week.
HPV 6&11 should make you think of?	Condyloma accuminata (genital warts)
Common warts aka?	Verruca Vulgaris

Parkland formula is used for what?	Burns
Parkland formula?	LR @ 4ml x kg x BSA burn (1/2 given in 1st 8 hr, rest over next 16 hr.)
Only childhood viral exanthem that starts on the trunk and spread to the face?	**Rose**ola 6th disease (Imagine rose on the trunk)
Roseola is caused by what HHV?	6&7
MC virus causing Hand-Foot-Mouth Dz?	Coxsackie A virus
3 Cs of measles/rubeola?	Cough, Corzy, conjunctivitis
Measles rash starts where?	At the hairline spreading down, fever is concurrent with the rash
How long does the measles rash last?	7 days
How long does German measles rash last?	3 days
Erythema Infectiosum (5th disease) is caused by which virus?	Parvovirus B19 (remember 5B19)
Erythema Infectiosum buzzwords?	Slapped cheek, lacy reticular rash on extremities (spares palms and soles)
Neonatal jaundice timeframes?	Physiological is first it occurs in the first 3-5 days. Breastfeeding jaundice next occurs in the first week of life. Breast milk jaundice occurs in the second week of life.
Perioral dermatitis is MC seen in?	Young woman

This rash **spares vermillion border**?	**Perioral** dermatitis
Perioral dermatitis treatment?	**Topical Metro**nidazole or Erythromycin
Inflammation of one or both corners of the mouth?	Angular cheilitis
Diaper dermatitis treatment?	Barrier creams, air drying or mild steroid
Erythematous rash with distinct satellite lesions, think?	Yeast Diaper candida
Yeasts Diaper candida treatment?	Clotrimazole ointment
Atopic dermatitis is likely a dysfunction of which protein in the epidermis?	Filaggrin protein
Cradle cap aka?	Seborrheic dermatitis
Seborrheic dermatitis treatment?	Selenium sulfide, Ketoconazole (shampoo or cream)
Pityriasis Rosea can mimic what other diseases?	Syphilis so do PRP if the pt is sexually active
Salmon colored macule?	Herold patch - Pityriasis Rosea
Is SJS more common in children or adults?	Children (TEN in adults)
Eczema treatment?	High strength topical steroids and antihistamine for itching
The Atopic triad is?	Asthma, Eczema and allergic rhinitis
What stimulates sebum production?	Androgens
Scabies is what type of hypersensitivity reaction?	Type 4
Male pattern baldness aka?	Androgenic alopecia

Small red spots in buccal mucosa with blue/white pale centers?	Koplik spots
Forchheimer's spots on the soft palate?	Rubella
Lymphadenopathy is associated with which viral exanthem?	Rubella/German measles
Sickle cell patients can get aplastic crisis from which exanthem?	5th slapped cheeks
Herpes Zoster/shingles are most contagious when?	The day before the rash appears
Dewdrop on a rose petal?	Vericella - chickenpox
MC sites of zoster eruption?	Thoracic and lumbar
Zoster infection pattern?	Dermatomal
Varicella rash starts where?	At the hairline and spreads down
Contact dermatitis treatment?	Avoid/remove the offending agent and topical corticosteroids are sufficient in most cases
Mild contact dermatitis?	Topical steroids and Diphenhydramine
Moderate to severe CD?	Benadryl and Prednisone
Drug skin eruption usually begins?	7-20 days after starting meds
Drug eruption is mediated by?	IgE
Pt with drug eruption that doesn't stop meds can develop?	DRESS Drug rash w eosinophilia and systemic symptoms. Generally starts w high fever, rash, inflammation of 1+organs

HSV is diagnosed with which smear?	Tzanck smear
Most sensitive test for Varicella-zoster?	PCR
Shingles treatment?	Acyclovir, Valacyclovir
Most painful type of all burns?	Superficial partial-thickness
Painful burn **with blisters**?	Superficial partial-thickness
Painful burn **without the blisters**?	Superficial burn
Burn with **blisters but no pain**?	Deep partial-thickness
Burn that's waxy white?	Full-thickness
DRESS timeframe?	2-6 weeks after drug initiation, LATER than other reactions
Urticarial rash?	Hives; a red, raised, and often itchy rash consistent with allergic reactions.
Pt with an urticarial rash after eating a fish?	Histamine fish poisoning
Minocycline for acne can cause?	Anaphylaxis
Burn treatment of fingers and toes?	They should be wrapped individually to prevent maceration
MC used abx for 2nd and 3rd-degree burns?	Silver sulfadiazine

Name the second-degree burns?	Superficial partial and deep partial (Dermis involved)
Treatment for tinea capitus?	Griseofulvin
Ringworm aka?	Tinea corporis
S or coma shaped burrow?	Scabies, contagious can be sexually transmitted
Scabies treatment?	Permethrin 5% cream
Painful rash on the face that started as tingling now full rash painful, blurry vision on that side?	Herpes zoster
Involvement of tip of the nose from herpes zoster?	Hutchinson sign. Pt can lose vision.
Herpes Zoster Treatment?	Acyclovir
Erysipelas - Bug?	GAS group a strep
Erysipelas vs cellulitis?	Erysipelas has well-marketed lines and its superficial where cellulitis doesn't and it's deeper. Both will be hot and may have a fever.
Hallmark feature of MRSA?	Abscess formation
The term used for genital warts?	Condyloma - cauliflower appearance
MC tx for Condyloma acuminate?	Cryotherapy
Physical exam reveals a petechial rash involving the palms and soles that **began on his wrists and ankles**?	Rocky Mountain Spotted Fever (RMSF)

What is the first-line antibiotic treatment for Rocky Mountain Spotted Fever?	Doxy
Yellow plaques on eyelids are called?	Xanthelasma
Hard, yellow masses found on tendons?	Xanthoma
MC form of primary irritant contact dermatitis?	Diaper dermatitis
The pink nodular, pearly white translucent appearance with inverted edges and telangiectatic vessels are typical of?	Basal cell carcinoma.
Actinic keratoses can be treated by cryotherapy or curettage. Extensive lesions can be treated with a topical agent such as?	5-fluorouracil
What's Acanthosis nigricans?	Dark hyperpigmentation around the neck, associated with insulin-resistant diabetes and PCOS
Tx for mild acne?	Topical retinoids
Tx for severe acne?	Isotretinoin
MC premalignant skin condition?	Actinic keratosis, MC is seen in fair-skinned elderly with prolonged sun exposure (face, around ears and neck)
Actinic keratosis dx?	Punch or shave biopsy

Actinic keratosis tx?	Observation, surgical (cryosurgery) medical (5-FU, Imiquimod)
Basal cell carcinoma description?	A flat, firm area with small **raised pearly papule** with central ulceration and raised **rolled borders**.
Basal cell carcinoma dx?	Punch or shave bx, basophilic cells on histology
BCC tx on the face?	Moh's microsurgery for facial BCC
Tinea versicolor is caused by?	Malassezia furfur
First-line treatment for keloids?	Corticosteroid injections
Pt with perioral dermatitis should avoid?	Topical steroids
Perioral dermatitis tx?	Topical metronidazole
MC form of bacteria causing common acne?	Propionibacterium
What antibiotic is commonly used to treat acne?	Erythromycin
Difference between rosacea and acne when comparing the rash?	Rosacea has an absence of comedones and the presence of Telangiectases
Cystic acne tx?	Tetracyclines, then oral retinoids - isotretinoin (Must obtain 2 pregnancy tests before starting it and monthly while on it)
Folliculitis is?	Infection of one or more of the hair follicles, characterized by papules and pustules

Folliculitis tx?	Mupirocin ointment and topical benzoyl peroxide cream are first-line, In more extensive cases, oral antibiotics may be necessary - dicloxacillin and cephalexin.
Pathogenesis of acne vulgaris?	Keratinocyte proliferation and decreased desquamation
First-line therapy for almost all patients with acne?	Topic retinoid
Isotretinoin may heighten feelings of?	Depression and suicidal thoughts
Rosacea treatment?	Metronidazole
Recommended to reduce recurrence in patients with rosacea?	Sunscreen
Erythema multiforme doesn't?	Itch
MC cause of Erythema multiforme?	HSV
An autoimmune attack against hair follicles is?	Alopecia areata. Oval shaped well-demarcated hair loss
Telogen effluvium is?	Premature shedding of hair in the resting phase
Typical male pattern baldness?	Androgenic alopecia
Androgenic alopecia tx?	Topical minoxidil and oral finasteride
MC cause of hair loss in women?	Androgenetic alopecia
Trichophyton rubrum, think?	Athlete's foot, onychomycosis
Ringworm tx?	Topical 1% clotrimazole cream

"Spaghetti and meatball" appearance in KOH?	Tinea versicolor
Epidermal/dermal cells with large hyperchromatic nuclei?	Actinic keratosis
Pearly, raised borders with telangiectasia and a central ulcer that may crust?	Basal cell carcinoma
Erythema Marginatum will have what kind of distribution?	Bathing suit distribution
Silvery plaques on extensor surfaces, think?	Psoriasis, tx with steroids
Erythematous scaling macule, think?	Actinic keratosis
Is ulcer or erosion the defect in the epidermis?	Erosions
How would you describe petechiae?	Flat and <4mm
Vesiculobullous means what?	Fluid-filled blisters
Bulla is?	Blister > 1cm raised contains serous fluid
Vesicle is?	Blister < 1cm raised contains fluid
Nodule is?	>1 cm firm/solid, like a ball on the skin
Papule is?	<1cm small raised no fluid inside
Pustules is?	<1cm full of pus

Macule is?	< 1cm flat (if you run your fingertips over with your eyes closed you can't feel the difference)
Patch is?	> 1 cm flat
Pruritic papules and plaques is a typical presentation of what?	Atopic Dermatitis
If the patient continues to scratch atopic dermatitis can turn into what?	Lichen Simplex Chronicus
Bleeding after the scale is scratched or picked in psoriasis is called what?	Auspitz sign
Stuck on waxy plaques, think?	Seborrheic keratosis (stuck on SK)
Inflammation around nails is called what?	Paronychia
Tender nodules in the axilla, think?	Hidradenitis suppurativa
Café au lait patches, think?	Neurofibromatosis

Good luck on your test! You have studied hard and I'm sure you will do just fine, remember "Thousand's and thousand's of students done this before you, so can you PERIOD". **PLEASE DO ME A HUGE FAVOR AND LEAVE AN AMAZON COMMENT FOR THE BOOK. THAT HELPS ME A LOT AND LET'S OTHER STUDENTS KNOW IF YOU FOUND THIS BOOK HELPFUL. THANK YOU!!!!!!**

Hematology

MC genetic disorder in Caucasians?	Hemochromatosis
MC race affected by **Thalassemia A**?	Asians (**A stands for Asians**)
MC race affected by Thalassemia B?	Mediterranean
MC cause of death in sickle cell patients?	Pulmonary issues
MC initial symptom of sickle cell patients?	Dactylitis
MC sickle cell is diagnosed by?	Hemoglobin electrophoresis
MC age group in ITP patients?	<40 years old
MC bleeding sites for Hemophilia A and B?	Joints (Likely ankle or a knee)
MC Hemophilia's A and B become symptomatic by what age?	Age 2
MC cancers causing fever of unknown origin?	Leukemia and Lymphoma
The most common cause of phlebitis?	Thrombophlebitis
MC cancer amongst the **15-19** years old?	Hodgkin's lymphoma
Reed Sterling Cells should make you think of what?	Hodgkin's lymphoma (**Have you REED about Hodgkin's**)
DVT Test of choice?	Doppler US
HITT syndrome often results in?	Loss of limb or life
Lymphoblast should make you think of?	ALL (LL for Lymph ALL)

Auer rods should make you think of?	AML
Myeloblasts should make you think of?	AML (M from AML for Myeloblasts)
What is leukocytosis with **the left shift**?	Most commonly, this means that there is an **infection** or inflammation present and the bone marrow is producing more WBCs and releasing them into the blood before they are fully mature.
Polycythemia Vera is?	**Increase in hemoglobin** above normal, too much RBC and erythro produces in the marrow
Treatment for VWD (von Willebrand disease)?	Desmopressin
Low molecular weight heparin is contraindicated in?	Low platelets and renal failure
Warfarin should be overlapped with heparin for at least how many days?	5 days and INR >2 at least 24 hours
PE anticoagulation treatment should be how long?	At least 6 months
MC anemia is?	Iron deficiency
If you hear PICA, think?	Iron deficiency
Iron deficiency anemia labs will show?	Low ferritin, high TIBC
Cause of physiologic anemia?	Decrease in erythropoiesis

MC cause of microcytic anemia?	Iron deficiency
MC cause of macrocytic anemia?	B12 and folate deficiency
Purely breastfed infants are at increased risk for what?	Iron deficiency
Sickle cell disease has what inheritance pattern?	Autosomal recessive (sickle cell kids love recess and auto- cars)
Sickle cell + salmonella?	Osteomyelitis
Sickle cell peripheral smear?	Target cells, **Howell-Jolly bodies** (there is nothing Jolly about sickle cell)
MC inherited bleeding disorder?	Von Willenbrands disease
Smooth beefy tongue, think?	B12 deficiency
MC childhood malignancy?	Leukemia
MC childhood leukemia?	ALL - Acute lymphoblastic leukemia (All kids)
ALL x-ray may show?	Mediastinal mass
Reed-Sternberg cells (owl's eye)?	Hodgkin's lymphoma
What are the B symptoms?	Fever, night sweats, and weight loss
Hemophilia A is a deficiency in which factor?	VIII (**8A, 9B**)

Hemophilia B is a deficiency in which factor?	IX
MC type of hemophilia?	Hemophilia A
Hemophilia A dx?	All normal but PTT, it will be increased
Desmopressin is not useful for which hemophilia?	Hemophilia B
MC regional lymphadenitis among children?	Cervical lymphadenitis
MC small vessel vasculitis in childhood?	Henoch-Schonlein purpura
MC bleeding disorder of childhood?	ITP
MC cause of thrombocytopenia?	ITP
CML age?	30-60
CML PE?	Splenomegaly (in Philly they have big spleens and WBC>100K)
Which chromosome is seen with **CML**?	**Philadelphia** chromosome
AML PE?	Hepatosplenomegaly, pt will have **FEVER**
Malignancy of lymphoid stem cell?	ALL
CLL age?	>60 **only one that starts after 60**
MC adult leukemia?	CLL

MC ACUTE leukemia in adults?	AML is most acute
Drugs that can cause G6PD?	Antimalarial, sulfa, nitro, fava beans
MC inherited cause of hypercoagulability?	Factor V Leiden mutation
ITP presentation?	Decreased platelet count with normal coagulation factors. CHILD 2-6 years old. Recent VIRAL infection, red spots on the skin, **PLATLET<50K**
ITP is MCC by?	Antiplatelet antibodies
ITP tx?	Observation, steroids, IVIG
How does the platelet count determine the treatment for ITP?	>50000 no treatment, 20000-50000: prednisone, <20000, iv immunoglobulin or Rhogam
Multiple myeloma blood smear?	**Rouleaux**
Multiple myeloma (MM) urine will show?	**Bance Jones protein**
MM is caused by?	Single **clone plasma** cell malignancy
Causes of sickling crisis?	Dehydration, hypoxia, acidosis
Sickle cell X-ray?	Pulm infiltrates
Which virus is associated with sickle cell?	Parvovirus B19

MCC of death in children with sickle cell?	S. pneumonia sepsis
Tx for sickle cell?	**Hydroxyurea** (fetal Hb), IVF, pain control, transfusion (if acute)
Labs in beta-thalassemia?	CODOcytes target
Beta Thalassemia tx?	Beta-thal major (**Cooley's**)- weekly transfusions and deferoxamine and other Fe chelating agents
For pernicious anemia do which test?	Schilling test
Elevated homocysteine and normal MMA, think?	Folate deficiency (Alcoholics)
Facial plethora, think?	aka ruddy cyanosis, **polycythemia Vera**
50% decrease in platelets, think?	HIT
Schistocytes are seen with?	TTP, HUS, DIC
Recurrent venous or arterial thrombosis at an early age?	Antiphospholipid syndrome associated with lupus, labs show thrombocytopenia, tx with anticoags
Thalassemia Dx?	Hemoglobin electrophoresis
Cooley's anemia (beta-thalassemia) age?	4-6 months
Glucose-6-phosphate dehydrogenase (G6PD) deficiency?	**Heinz bodies, bite cells (On that G6 plane I was taking a BITE and had some Heinz Ketchup)**

Howell-Jolly bodies?	Sickle cell
Rouleaux formation of RBCs - diagnosis?	Multiple myeloma
Hallmark of acute leukemia is?	Pancytopenia with circulating blasts
Heparin MOA?	Inhibits thrombin by activating antithrombin III and inhibits factor Xa
The hallmark of aplastic anemia is?	Pancytopenia (a condition that occurs when a person has low counts for all three types of blood cells: red blood cells, white blood cells, and platelets.)
MC cause of B12 deficiency?	Pernicious anemia
MC population affected with B12 deficiency?	Vegans (Any questions with vegan pt think B12 deficiency)
MC risk factors of B12 deficiency?	Increased risk of gastric cancer
MC location of bacterial overgrowth in B12 deficiency?	Terminal ileum
MC sites for bone marrow biopsy?	Pelvis and sternum
Normochromic normocytic anemia, think?	Anemia of chronic disease
Failure to thrive in the baby is seen with which thalassemia?	Beta thalassemia MAJOR
What causes fatigue?	Anemia most likely
How do we treat hemolytic transfusion reaction?	Stop the transfusion and hydrate the patient

What's neutropenia?	Low WBC, indicates infection
Teardrop cells are seen with?	ALL - Acute lymphoblastic leukemia
HgB>18.5 is indicative of?	Polycythemia Vera
Polycythemia Vera is characterized by an abnormality in which cells?	Clonal stem cells
Presence of **JAK2** mutation, think?	**Polycythemia Vera (Poly and Jack)**
Pt reports that they are feeling itchy **(pruritus) after the shower**, think?	**Polycythemia Vera**
What physical findings can be found in patients with polycythemia Vera?	Facial flushing and splenomegaly
What is the treatment for polycythemia Vera?	Phlebotomy to keep hct<45%
In acute leukemia, the Blasts will be?	>20%
What are the 3 phases of CML?	Chronic, accelerated and blast crisis
Name the medication that can treat CML?	Gleevac (Imatinib)
Question asked about the child with leukemia, they most likely have?	ALL - Acute lymphoblastic leukemia
What causes ALL?	Radiation, Chemo, and genetic disorder
Gingival hyperplasia, think?	ALL - Acute lymphoblastic leukemia

PT with ALL will likely show what level of WBC on CBC?	High 50's and blasts will be in high 80's
Testicular enlargement is common in pt with?	ALL - Acute lymphoblastic leukemia
Does chemo cross the blood-brain barrier?	It does not
Smudge cells are indicative of which leukemia?	**CLL**
Hodgkin's lymphoma are malignant cells derived from?	B lymphocytes
Hodgkin's lymphoma presents at what age?	teens and again in 55+
Painless enlarged lymph node in the neck, think?	Hodgkin's lymphoma
What is the mean age of the patient with multiple myeloma?	The mean age is 62
What is the average survival of patients with multiple myeloma?	The average is 7 years
Christmas disease is aka which hemophilia?	Hemophilia B
Lytic lesions on skull x-ray, think?	Multiple myeloma
ADAMTS13, think?	**TTP** - Thrombotic Thrombocytopenic Purpura
RBC looks like a **stack of coins**, think?	Multiple myeloma
Hyper segmented neutrophils are seen with?	Folate and B12 deficiencies

What is a normal MCV?	80-100
MCV under 80 indicates?	Microcytic anemia
What are some examples of microcytic anemia?	Lead, Thalassemia and most commonly Iron deficiency
Where does the folate absorption take place?	At the jejunum
Glossitis is associated with B12 or folate deficiency?	B12
The question talks about the patient with ice cravings, they most likely have what?	Iron deficiency
The question talks about eating clay and the patient has angular cheilitis, think?	Iron deficiency
Plummer-Vinson syndrome is an associate with which anemia?	Iron deficiency
What is the only lab value that will be increased in iron deficiency?	TIBC, rest of them are down
Which vitamin increases iron absorption?	Vit C
Basophilic stippling, think?	**Lead poisoning**
Succimer is a medication used to treat which anemia?	**Lead poisoning** anemia
G6PD can be seen with what kind of jaundice?	Neonatal
Question talks about H-shaped vertebrae, think?	Sickle cell

What is a heparin overdose antidote?	Protamine
Does PTT or PT measure the Extrinsic pathway?	PT
What is the warfarin overdose antidote?	Vit K
Question talks about antibodies vs ADAMTS13, think?	TTP - Thrombotic Thrombocytopenic Purpura
What is the treatment for TTP?	Plasmapheresis
How to tell if the patient has HUS and not TTP?	HUS patients will not have neurologic signs and fever
If the child presents with diarrhea and renal failure, think?	HUS - Hemolytic Uremic syndrome
What patient population is mostly affected by HUS?	Kids
If the question talks about the patient that is bleeding from all sites including IV puncture sites, think?	DIC - Disseminated Intravascular Coagulation
What is the only lab value that will be decreased in a DIC?	Fibrinogen, rest are up
What kind of purpura can be seen with children after the URI?	ITP - Idiopathic Thrombocytopenic Purpura
Will the patient have splenomegaly in ITP?	They will not, that is with TTP
MC type of non-Hodgkin's lymphoma?	Diffuse large B cell
Non-Hodgkin's lymphoma biopsy will show?	Starry sky pattern

Infectious Disease

What are the universal signs of infection?	Fever, pain, and swelling
Yeast and mold are what?	Fungi (Yeast is a single cell and mold is dysmorphic)
How do viruses replicate?	By controlling the host cell metabolic mechanism
Viruses lack which enzymes?	Protein synthesizing enzymes
Bacteria are what kind of cells?	Simple prokaryotic cell no nucleus and organelles
Bacteria have what kind of DNA?	Circular
What shape are cocci?	Round
If you hear gram-positive cocci in chains, think?	Strep
If you hear gram-positive cocci in clusters, think?	Staph
If you hear gram-positive bacilli, think?	Clostridia (Bacilli rods are elongated)
What does Aspergillus need in order to grow?	It needs spores
What's the difference between yeast and mold?	Yeast is tissue and mold is the environment
When you hear Protozoal, think?	Parasites

Protozoal is what kind of cell organism?	Single-cell
Protozoa found in red blood cells is what?	Malaria
Protozoal is most stable in which form?	Cyst form
Most antibiotics are produced from what?	Fungi
Strep Viridans and strep bovis can be treated with?	PCN G
Neisseria Meningitis can be treated with?	PCN G
Bacteriocidal vs Bacteriostatic MOA (mechanism of action)?	Bacteriocidal kills bacteria and bacteriostatic inhibit the growth)
What are the 5 sites of antibiotic action in bacteriostatic?	1. Inhibition of cell wall synthesis 2. Inhibition of protein synthesis 3. Inhibition of DNA and RNA synthesis 4. Inhibition of folate synthesis 5. Membrane disruption
What is bioavailability?	The term used for absorption of the medication
A measure of the degree of pathogenicity of a microorganism is termed?	Virulence
Folliculitis is caused by which organism?	Staph Aureus
What is folliculitis?	Hair follicle infection

Most common (MC) bug causing the Impetigo?	Staph Aureus
Impetigo buzzword?	Honey-colored crusted
Impetigo treatment?	Bactroban 2% ointment if extensive Keflex
Erysipelas is caused by which bug?	GAS group a strep
Erysipelas vs cellulitis?	Erysipelas has well-marked lines and its superficial where cellulitis doesn't and it's deeper. Both will be hot and may have a fever.
Hallmark feature of MRSA?	Abscess formation
What is cellulitis?	Infection of subcutaneous and connective tissue.
What are the symptoms of cellulitis?	Fever, Increased WBC, chills, and warm to touch.
The most common bug causing cellulitis?	Staph Aureus
Herpes Zoster/shingles are most contagious when?	The day before the rash appears
Painful rash on the face that started as tingling now with a full rash that is painful, this describes?	Herpes zoster
What is the sign called that involves the tip of the nose from herpes zoster?	Hutchinson sign. Patients can lose vision.
Herpes Zoster Treatment?	Acyclovir (antiviral drug)

Dewdrop on a rose petal, think?	Vericella - chickenpox
MC sites of zoster eruption?	Thoracic and lumbar
Zoster infection aka shingles has what kind of pattern?	Dermatomal
Varicella rash starts where?	At the hairline and spreads down
Warts are what kind of papules?	Hyperkeratotic
HSV is diagnosed with which smear?	Tzanck smear
Most sensitive test for Varicella-zoster?	PCR
MC virus causing Hand-Foot-Mouth Dz?	Coxsackie A virus
Small domed papules with the umbilicated center, think?	Molluscum Contagiosum
Molluscum Contagiosum tx?	Self-limiting (it's a pox virus)
Molluscum Contagiosum buzzword?	Dome-shaped, flesh-colored, central umbilication
3 Cs of measles/rubeola?	Cough, Corzy, conjunctivitis
Measles rash starts where?	At the hairline spreading down, fever is concurrent with a rash
How long does the measles rash last?	7 days

How long does German measles rash last?	3 days
MC virus that causes Rubella/German measles?	Togavirus
MC organism in acute osteomyelitis?	S. Aureus
How do we acquire osteomyelitis?	Bacteria from the blood gets into the bone.
How long will it take for osteomyelitis to be seen on an x-ray?	4 weeks (MRI is 1st choice for imaging)
Osteomyelitis after puncture wound is caused by which organism?	Pseudomonas (Runner steps on something and bacteria from the sole of the shoes gets into the bloodstream)
Erythema Infectiosum (5th disease) is caused by which virus?	Parvovirus B19 (remember 5B19)
Erythema Infectiosum buzzwords?	Slapped cheek, lacy reticular rash on extremities (spares palms and soles)
Septic arthritis is an infection of what?	Joints it's more painful than osteomyelitis
The most common organism causing septic arthritis in children?	HiB Haemophilus influenza
The most common organism causing septic arthritis in adults?	Neisseria gonorrhea
Which cells in our body are responsible for making antibodies?	B-cells (derived from bone marrow)

A foreign substance that triggers immune response is called?	Antigen
What are the 4 types of T-cells?	Helper, cytotoxic, suppressor and killer
Cytotoxic T-cells CD8 do what?	Recognize epitopes and kill
What do suppressor T-cells do?	Modulate and terminate immune response
Antibodies are found where?	In circulation and on the surface of B-cells
IgE is responsible for what?	Allergic response
In the earliest response do we see IgG or IgM first?	IgM
Is staph aureus catalase + or -?	Its catalase positive. Strep is catalase negative
Pregnant women exposed to parvovirus can develop?	Hydrops Fetalis
Treatment of choice for strep pharyngitis?	PCN VK
When can patients with strep return to the school?	After being on ABX for 24hr.
TB clinical symptoms?	Fever, night sweats, weight loss, malaise, cough
TB x-ray findings?	Ghon complex
TB dx?	CXR, Acid-fast bacilli, PCR, PPD skin test

MC bug in bacterial sinusitis?	S. pneumonia
Strep pharyngitis should always be treated for how long?	10 days to prevent rheumatic fever
Otitis Media treatment?	Amoxicillin
MC bug causing Otitis media?	S. Pneumonia
OM treatment if the patient has a PCN allergy?	Ceftriaxone, Cefdinir
What's considered recurrent OM?	3+ episodes of AOM in 6 months or 4+ in one year
Acute sinusitis test of choice?	CT
When do we give ABX for sinusitis?	If symptoms are present for >10 days (<7 is viral)
MC bug in chronic sinusitis?	S. Aureus
MC virus that causes the common cold?	Rhinovirus
Enterovirus most commonly affects what?	GI tract
HSV 1 and 2 affect what?	HSV1 effects eyes/mouth and HSV2 affects genitals
Which vaccine can help prevent epiglottis?	Hib
Think epiglottitis if the child presents with?	Drooling, sitting in the sniffing tripod position and leaning forward

3 Ds of Epiglottitis?	Dysphagia, drooling and distress
Inspiratory stridor think?	Epiglottitis
Epiglottitis diagnostic test?	Lateral neck x-ray showing the Thumbprint sign
MC cause of croup?	Parainfluenza virus
Barking cough, think?	Croup
Epiglottitis is most commonly caused by which bug?	HIB-Haemophilus influenza
Steeple sign on x-ray?	Croup
Drug of choice for treatment of pertussis?	Macrolide (Azithromycin)
Bordatella pertussis is also know as?	Whopping cough
Bordatella pertussis can't survive without?	The host
Bordatella pertussis is gram what?	Gram negative coccobacilli
Which stage of whooping cough is most contagious?	Catarrhal stage
S. Pneumoniae gram stain?	Gram + cocci in pairs
MC cause of viral PNA in infants	RSV

RSV presentation?	A wet cough, intercostal retractions, scattered crackles, expiratory wheezes bilat. decreased PO intake, fever.
MC cause of lower respiratory tract infection?	RSV
MC symptoms of CAP (Community-acquired pneumonia)?	Cough with purulent sputum, fever, and dyspnea
Which virus can be caused by deer mouse feces?	Hantavirus
What are the only bacteria with a cell wall?	Mycoplasma
Mycoplasma causes what?	Walking pneumonia
Mycoplasma treatment?	Azithromycin
MC PNA bug?	Strep Pneumo
CAP vs. HCAP run?	Drip score >4 it's HCAP
PNA site of care?	CURB65
Mycoplasma pneumonia is usually seen in which group of people?	College and military
Legionella is associated with?	Cooling towers, AC, contaminated water supplies
MC bug in alcoholics with PNA?	Klebsiella

Aspiration PNA bug?	Anaerobes
Rusty sputum sample?	S. Pneumo
Currant jelly sputum sample?	Klebsiella
Foul-smelling sputum sample?	Anaerobes
Hyponatremia is seen with which type of pneumonia?	Legionella
To grow legionella which agar is used?	Charcoal yeast agar
Dx of TB?	Acid-fast smear and sputum culture x 3 days: AFB cultures GOLD STANDARD
Reactivation TB will be seen in what part of the lungs in the CXR?	Apical (upper lobe)
Tx for TB?	RIPE (rifampin, isoniazid, pyrazinamide, ethambutol)
Side effects of Rifampin?	Turns urine orange
Neisseria meningitis is gram what?	Gram negative diplococci
MC causes of bacterial meningitis in neonates?	Group B Strep, E. coli, and Listeria
MC causes of bacterial meningitis in children 1m to 18 years old?	Neisseria meningitis

MC causes of bacterial meningitis in adults?	S. Pneumo
Bacterial meningitis treatment for neonates?	Ampicillin
Bacterial meningitis treatment for 1m-18y?	Ceftriaxone and Vanco
Bacterial meningitis treatment for adults?	Ceftriaxone + ampicillin + Vanco
Signs of meningitis?	High fever, stiff neck, drowsiness, and intense headache; may progress to coma and death within hours of onset
4 T of tetanus?	Trismus- lockjaw, Tetany- muscle spasm, Twitching and tightness
Cause of meningitis in HIV pt?	Cryptococcus neoformans
Klebsiella pneumonia is seen in which type of patients?	Alcoholics
Cat scratch which bug is involved?	Bartonella (Cat from the Bar)
What's the treatment for septic arthritis caused by Neisseria G.?	Ceftriaxone
Treatment for non-pregnant patients with UTI?	Fluoroquinolones
Dog bites treatment?	Augmentin (Auuu for Augmentin that dog bite hurts)
Bacterial meningitis CSF will show?	Increased WBC, Increased Protein and decreased glucose (Bacterial meningitis doesn't like sugar glucose down)

Viral meningitis CSF will show?	increased lymphocytes, normal glucose
TB causes what kind of meningitis?	Atypical onset 1-2 weeks
When to start abx in meningitis?	W/in 20 min
MCC of fungal meningitis?	Cryptococcus - India ink stain
Cryptococcus neoformans is found where?	In the dust of bird droppings
MC cause of chronic diarrhea in AIDs patients?	Cryptosporidium (HIV think Crypto)
MCC of Otitis externa?	Pseudomonas
What is encephalitis?	Viral infection of brain parenchyma
What is the sign called that is seen in meningitis patients when they can't straighten the knee with hip flexion?	Kernig's sign
What is the sign called that is seen in meningitis patients where neck flexion causes them to bend their knee/hips?	Brusinski
MOA of Aminoglycosides?	Inhibits protein synthesis
MOA of Monobactams?	Inhibits Cell wall synthesis
MOA of carbapenems?	Inhibits Cell wall synthesis

MCC C diff?	Abx like clindamycin (Clinda not Cipro) tx metro for mild Vanco for severe (PO not IV)
MCC of bacterial enteritis in the US?	Campylobacter jejuni - tx with fluids if severe erythromycin
MOA of clindamycin?	Binds to 50s ribosomal subunits to inhibit bacterial protein synthesis
MOA of Metronidazole?	Works to disturb bacterial DNA
MOA of vancomycin?	Binds D-ala D-ala groups, cell wall inhibitor
Injecting vancomycin to fast can cause what?	Redman syndrome
Will the use of narcotics cause diarrhea or constipation?	Constipation
How do we treat MRSA, what's the first choice drug?	1. Vanco 2. Daptomycin 3. Linezolid 4. TMP/SMZ
Which meds cover strep?	PCN G, PCN VK, Ampicillin, Amoxicillin, Pip/tazo
If the question stem talks about hot tub exposure most likely bug involved?	Pseudomonas
Pseudomonas coverage first choice med?	Pip/Tazo (P for P)
AZOLES like Clotrimazole and fluconazole are what kind of agents?	Antifungal (moa cell wall inhibitors)
Which azole can cause QT prolongation?	Fluconazole

UTI medication of choice?	Macrobid (Nitrofurantoin)
Avoid Macrobid of patients GFR is what?	Under 60 (GFR<60 indicated kidney damage)
Which medication used for UTI treatment can turn urine brown?	Macrobid (Nitrofurantoin)
Postcoital UTI tx?	Single-dose TMP-SMX or cephalexin may reduce the frequency of UTI in sexually active women
MC cause of recurrent cystitis in men?	Chronic bacterial prostatitis
Children with measles should be given which vitamin?	Vit A decreases mortality
MC vector for the Zika virus?	Aedes mosquito, single-stranded RNA flavivirus
Constitutional symptoms are?	Fever, sweats, myalgia, malaise, and pain
Which HIV Medication can cause bone marrow suppression?	Zidovudine
HIV med causing stones?	Indinavir
MC nosocomial infection?	#1 UTI, #2 HAP
MC cause of UTI?	E.Coli
Bells palsy is associated with witch HSV?	HSV1

MC cause of encephalitis?	HSV
HSV is diagnosed with which smear?	Tzanck smear
Most sensitive test for Varicella-zoster?	PCR
Encephalitis symptoms?	Fever, delirium, dementia, seizures, palsies, paralysis (FEVER+AMS)
HSV encephalitis treatment?	Requires immediate IV acyclovir
Syphilis is what?	Spirochete sexually transmitted, Treponemal pallidum
Syphilis presentation?	Painless, red, raised, firm ulcer >1cm - CHANCRE
Syphilis dx?	VDRL and RPR
Syphilis tx?	PCN G, follow the RPR and VDRL titers
Chancroid is hard to dx because of difficulty isolating what in the lab?	Haemophilus ducreyi (think HD-Chancroid)
Chancroid presentation?	Painful Genital ulcers have an erythematous base; the borders are clearly demarcated and the ulcer is usually covered with a gray or yellow purulent exudate and bleeds when scraped.
MC serious complication of STD?	PID

PID presentation?	Pelvic/lower abdominal pain, dysuria, dyspareunia, vaginal discharge, N/V, fever
PID PE will show?	+ Chandelier sign= cervical motion tenderness
PID tx?	Ceftriaxone IM (gon/chlam) + doxycycline
Chancroid vs Chancre?	Chancre (syphilis) is painless!
Chancroid tx?	Azithromycin 1gr PO single dose or Ceftriaxone 250mg IM
Lymphogranuloma venereum is a genital ulcer disease caused by?	L1, L2, and L3 serovars of Chlamydia trachomatis
Diagnosis of LGV?	Men who have sex with men (MSM) who present with proctitis, enlarged inguinal lymph nodes, and the presence of anorectal ulcers
LGV tx?	Doxycycline
MCC of reactive arthritis?	Chlamydia
MC STI in the USA?	Chlamydia
When testing for gonorrhea also test for?	Chlamydia
Treatment for gonorrhea?	Ceftriaxone 250mg IM
MCC of cervicitis?	Chlamydia

Treatment for Chlamydia?	Azithromycin 1gr PO single dose or Doxy
Painful, grouped vesicles on an erythematous base, think?	Herpes Simplex
The term used for genital warts?	Condyloma - cauliflower appearance
Condyloma accuminata is caused by?	HPV 6 and 11
MC tx for Condyloma accuminata?	Cryotherapy
Gardnerella vaginalis think?	Bacterial vaginosis (BV)
BV symptoms?	A fishy odor that's the worst after sex
BV discharge will be?	Thin white/grey fishy smell
BV wet prep will show?	Clue cells
BV pH will be?	between 5 and 6 (BV pH 5-6 and Trich is 6-7)
BV tx?	Metro for 7 days
MCC of GYN visits?	Vaginitis
Vaginitis dx?	Wet-prep
Trichomoniasis is usually transmitted how?	STI

Flagellated protozoan think?	Trichomoniasis
Trichomoniasis signs and symptoms?	Frothy yellow-green discharge, strawberry cervix, dysuria, dyspareunia
Trichomoniasis dx?	Wet-prep (motile trichomonads, movement of flagella)
Trichomoniasis tx?	Single dose of Metronidazole 2 gr
MC agent in Vaginal Candidiasis	Candida Albicans
Vaginal candidiasis presentation?	White thick clumpy discharge - cottage cheese
Vaginal candidiasis wet prep will show?	Branching hyphae and spores, pH of 4-5
Vaginal candidiasis tx?	Single dose Fluconazole PO
Lice treatment?	Permethrin 1% shampoo, wash clothing and bedding
What's the dysentery diarrhea?	Bloody and fever
Norovirus is MC cause of?	Gastroenteritis in adults in the USA- think cruise ships, hospitals, restaurants.
Vomiting is predominant sx in most?	Noninvasive diarrhea
MC cause of diarrhea in children?	Rotavirus
Noninvasive (Enterotoxin) Infectious Diarrhea?	Noninvasive= vomiting, watery, voluminous, no fecal WBCs or

	blood (if it had blood that would be dysentery)
Staphylococcus incubation period?	W/in 6h. Food contamination is MCC. Dairy, meat, mayo, and eggs.
How long does staph diarrhea last?	Self-limiting 1-2 days. treatment is supportive
Which bug can cause diarrhea after consuming the fried rice?	Bacillus Cereus
"Rice-water stools" severe dehydration?	Vibreo Cholera
Vibreo Cholera tx?	Fluid replacement is the mainstay
MC cause of traveler's diarrhea?	Enterotoxigenic E.Coli
Symptoms of E coli?	Abrupt onset of watery diarrhea, cramps, and vomiting
Management of E coli?	Fluids first +/_ pepto, if severe fluroquinalones
Invasive infectious diarrhea presentation?	High fevers, + blood & fecal leukocytes, not as voluminous (large intestine), mucus, NO anti-motility drugs to pts c invasive diarrhea (may cause toxicity from bacteria)
MC bugs that cause infectious diarrhea?	Shigella, Y. enterocolitica, salmonella, enterohemorrhagic e coli, c. enteritis
MC cause of bacterial enteritis in the USA.	Campylobacter Enteritis.

How's diarrhea present in campylobacter enteritis?	First watery than bloody
Campylobacter enteritis is contracted from?	Poultry (turkey)
Campylobacter enteritis treatment?	Erythromycin
Shigella sx?	Crampy lower abdominal pain, fever, tenesmus, explosive watery diarrhea > mucoid, bloody
Children with shigella can get?	Febrile seizures
Dx of shingles?	Stool cx; fecal WBC/RBC; Sigmoidoscopy: punctuate areas of ulcerations, WBC>50
Treatment for shigella?	Fluids first if severe TMP/SMT (Bactrim)
Pea soup stools?	Salmonella
Tx for salmonella?	Fluids if severe fluroquinalones (floxacins) ciprofloxacin
MC cause of gastritis?	H.Pylori
Dx of gastritis?	Endoscopy= GOLD STANDARD
Tx for gastritis?	CAP for H pylori-positive (amoxicillin, clarithromycin, and PPI think CAP for treatment)
"Backpackers diarrhea"?	Giardia Lamblia

Giardia Lamblia treatment?	Metronidazole (Flagyl)
Frothy, greasy diarrhea?	Giardia Lamblia
Giardia Lamblia dx?	Trophozites in stool
HIV is caused by?	Retrovirus
Kaposi sarcoma CD4 counts?	200-500
CMV CD4 count?	<50
List some first-gen cephalosporins?	Cephalexin, cefadroxil and cefazolin
Carbapenems have what major side effects?	They can reduce the seizure threshold
Don't use Doxycycline in which patients?	Kids <8 and pregnant patients or patients with liver issues. Also, it can cause teeth discoloration
Which medication can cause cartilage damage?	Fluoroquinolones
If you prescribe Metronidazole to patients warn them not to use what with this medication?	EtOH
Which medication inhibits folic acid synthesis?	Bactrim
Which medication is used in life threatening fungal infections?	Amphotericin B

Which disease can be transferred by rabbits?	Tularemia
Tularemia treatment?	Streptomycin
Prisoner drinking wine now with ptosis, blurry vision, diplopia?	Botulism tx airway they can die w/in 6h
Floppy baby syndrome is seen with?	Botulism (ingestion of honey under 1 year of age)
MCC of Lyme Disease?	Borrelia burgdorferi - that is spread by the vector Ixodes (deer) tick
Lyme disease is associated with which erythema?	Erythema migrans. Expanding, a warm, annular, erythematous rash with central clearing
Tx for Lyme disease?	Doxy, For children under 8 and pregnant patients tx is Amoxicillin?
Physical exam reveals a petechial rash involving the palms and soles that began on his wrists and ankles?	Rocky Mountain Spotted Fever (RMSF)
What is the first-line antibiotic treatment for Rocky Mountain Spotted Fever?	Doxy
MCC of death in rocky mountain spotted fever?	Myocarditis
Pinworm parasite?	Enterobius vermicularis
MC parasitic intestinal infection?	Pinworms

Pinworm test?	Cellophane tape test
Pinworm treatment?	Albendazole
Posterior cervical lymphadenopathy, think?	EBV (MONO)
Prophylaxis for CD4<100?	Bactrim
Rocky Mountain spotted fever will present with what kind of rash?	Rash that begins on wrists and ankles (Tx with Doxy)
Tendon rupture is seen with the use of which abx?	Quinolones (floxacins)
Ototoxicity is the side effect of which abx?	Aminoglycosides

Good luck on your test! You have studied hard and I'm sure you will do just fine, remember "Thousand's and thousand's of students done this before you, so can you PERIOD". **PLEASE DO ME A HUGE FAVOR AND LEAVE AN AMAZON COMMENT FOR THE BOOK. THAT HELPS ME A LOT AND LET'S OTHER STUDENTS KNOW IF YOU FOUND THIS BOOK HELPFUL. THANK YOU!!!!!!**

OB/GYN

What are the side effects of progestin?	Breast tenderness, Nausea, Cramps, Anxiety, Depression, Irritability
Which drug is used for the prevention of breast cancer recurrence?	Tamoxifen
The anorexic athletic patient, that is on progestin therapy will likely have what kind of menorrhea?	Hypomenorrhea
Patients that are taking Progestin are at increased risk of?	CVD, stroke, DVT/PE, Breast cancer, MI
Patients that are taking estrogen are at increased risk of?	DVT, stroke, Triglycerides increase
Ovulation induction medication?	Clomid (take in during the follicular phase)
The most common cause of ovulatory failure that causes infertility?	PCOS
RUQ pain, tenderness, and Increased **LFT's** think?	Fitzhugh-Curtis Syndrome (a complication of acute PID)
Treatment for pregnant patients with Chlamydia?	Azithromycin
What is the most common (MC) reportable STD?	Chlamydia
MC germ cell tumor in OB/GYN?	Teratoma

What is the name of the cyst that can cause a delay in menses?	Corpus Luteal cyst
MC type of ovarian cyst?	Follicular cyst aka simple cyst
How would you describe a Follicular cyst?	Unilateral, fluid-filled, usually resolve in 2-3 weeks
Which polyp can cause post-coital bleeding?	Cervical polyp
What's the Nabothian cyst?	The common cervical lesion, asymptomatic <1cm
Describe the Bartholin's abscess?	Bartholin's cyst that got infected. Pea-shaped glands located on each side of the vaginal opening that secrete fluid to lubricate the vagina
Name the 3 types of breast cancer?	Lobular, ductal and inflammatory
What are the protective factors for breast cancer?	Late menarche and early menopause
What is the most common benign tumor of the breast?	Fibroadenoma
What is the most common location of breast cancer?	Upper outer quadrant
Which drug can cause the failure of OCPs?	Rifampin
Persistent acne and hirsutism are a red flag for what?	Hyperandrogenism (**PCOS**, tumors)
Unilateral nipple discharge is more commonly associated with what?	Intraductal papilloma

Snowstorm pattern on the US, think?	Hydatidiform mole
What is the most common type of Gestational Trophoblastic Disease?	Hydatidiform mole
Procidentia of the uterus refers to?	Complete prolapse of the uterus
Which hormone is dominant in the luteal phase of menstruation?	Progesterone
The most common type of Gyn malignancy?	Endometrial cancer
What is a timeframe for clinical breast exam screening?	Clinical breast exam every 3 years in women age 20-39 years, annually after age 40
(hCG) the assay can detect the presence of hCG as early as?	5 days post-conception
What is a test of choice for uterine leiomyomas (fibroids)?	The pelvic US
What tocolytic agent is used in the treatment of pre-term labor to suppress uterine activity?	Magnesium sulfate
What is the most common cause of postpartum fever/sepsis?	Endometritis (think about this first if the patient has a reported postpartum fever)
Retraction of the delivered head against the maternal perineum describes what sign?	Turtle sign - the sign of shoulder dystocia
What is the triad of pre-eclampsia?	Hypertension, proteinuria, edema with onset after 20 weeks of gestation.

Treatment of Fibrocystic breast disease?	NSAIDs - Heat or ice - Supportive bra - Decrease caffeine/chocolate
How would you describe what is an Incompetent Cervix?	It's a recurrent 2nd-semester miscarriage
Diagnoses of the incompetent cervix are made with which imaging modality?	Ultrasound - will see **funneling of the cervix**
What is the treatment for incompetent cervix?	Treated with cervical cerclage placed at 14-16 weeks and removed at 36 weeks to allow for delivery
Management of ASC-US ages 25-29?	Preferred—Repeat Pap test in 12 months
Management of LSIL ages 25-29	Repeat Pap test in 12 months, if HPV + colposcopy is acceptable
Mildly friable, erythematous cervix with no active discharge describes what?	Cervicitis
The presence of sterile pyuria in a sexually active individual is most commonly associated with what?	Chlamydia
How do you cure a woman with preeclampsia?	Delivering the fetus will cure preeclampsia
Expulsion of all or part of the products of conception before 20 weeks of gestation describes what?	Spontaneous abortion
To improve the poor contractions during the delivery we can give which medication?	IV Pitocin

What are the classic features of an ectopic pregnancy?	Abdominal pain, bleeding, and **adnexal mass** in a pregnant woman
Ring of a fire sign is seen with what?	**Adnexal mass** with gestational sac outside of the uterus
Beta HCG is > 1,500, but no fetus in utero seen in the US, think?	Ectopic pregnancy
When is the Methotrexate given for ectopic pregnancy?	If beta HCG < 5,000, ectopic mass is < 3.5 cm, no fetal heart tones, no folate supplements. If any of these are present do salpingectomy.
What is gestational hypertension?	BP > 150/90 after 20 weeks into the pregnancy that resolves 12 weeks postpartum
Death of the fetus before 20 weeks of gestation, with products of conception remaining intrauterine, describes what?	Missed abortion
Pre-eclampsia is an indication of what?	Immediate delivery, but not necessarily by cesarean section.
What medication is used in the emergency contraception pill?	Levonorgestrel
When is the luteal phase of the menstrual cycle?	Days 15-28
Name some contraindications to OCP use?	OCP's should not be used in women > 35 years of age that are smokers, patients with a history of blood clots, breast cancer or migraines with aura

Which OCP is safe in lactation - can be used in breastfeeding women?	Mini Pill progestin only
Name some Estrogenic side effects?	Bloating, nausea/vomiting, breast fullness, breakthrough bleeding, irritability, headache, HTN
Name one Progestin-only IUD?	Mirena
What is recommended for the use in emergency contraception?	Continue to recommend a levonorgestrel emergency contraceptive (Plan B One-Step, etc.) within 3 days of unprotected sex or prescribe Ella (ulipristal) within 5 days. Consider a copper IUD within 5 days if the woman also wants long-lasting contraception. It's the most effective emergency contraceptive.
Sexual gratification attained by exposing genitals to unsuspecting strangers describes what disorder?	Exhibitionistic disorder
Primary hypogonadism will have what FSH/testosterone labs?	High FSH and low testosterone
Luteal phase (day 21) progesterone level is checked for ovulation - if the progesterone level is under 3 ng/ml on day 21 then you know that the patient?	Didn't ovulate

What hormone would be most definitive in diagnosing menopause in a 54-year-old female with amenorrhea?	FSH levels > 30
A severe, sometimes disabling extension of premenstrual syndrome (PMS) that's causing marked disruption in functioning is called what?	Premenstrual dysphoric disorder (PMDD)
How do we treat vulvar cancer?	With radiation
These cysts are presumed to be malignant until proven otherwise?	Postmenopausal ovarian cysts
Management of simple cysts greater> 7 cm?	For simple cysts, greater > 7 cm, further imaging with MRI or surgical assessment is mandated as, due to their large size, these cysts cannot be reliably assessed by ultrasound alone.
What are the risk factors for PID?	Having multiple sexual partners, using intrauterine devices, and having a prior PID
PID treatment medications?	Ceftriaxone (IM) and Doxycycline (PO)
What are the sequelae of PID?	Infertility, ectopic pregnancy, chronic pelvic pain, and recurrent episodes of PID
How is the diagnosis of PID made?	Clinical findings suggested by direct abdominal tenderness, **cervical motion tenderness**, and adnexal tenderness plus 1 or more of the following: temperature > 38°C, WBC count > 10,000/mm3 or pelvic abscess

	found by manual examination or ultrasonography
What must be considered in a female patient complaining of feeling a **bulge in the vagina and pelvic pressure?**	Uterine prolapse - Cystocele
Treatment options for endometriosis?	NSAIDs - Oral contraceptives - Danazol - GnRH agonists
Increased levels of endometrial prostaglandin production are seen with?	Primary dysmenorrhea
Treatment for primary dysmenorrhea?	NSAIDs
Name two primary amenorrhea causes?	Hypothalamic hypogonadism which is common in runners and eating disorders seen with the young woman.
What is the MOA of Methotrexate?	Folic acid antagonist - inhibits DNA synthesis
The histologic finding of plasma cells in the endometrial stroma is indicative of what?	Chronic endometritis can be linked to infertility.
Maternal hypotension, secondary to decreased systemic vascular resistance, is a complication associated with what during the delivery?	Epidural and spinal anesthesia, though it is a bit more common with spinal anesthesia.
Fever and chills are not a sign of what when comes to the labor?	Active labor, its likely infection.
Prior cesarean section is a risk factor for?	Uterine rupture

Screening for group B streptococcus is performed between which weeks during the pregnancy?	35 and 37 weeks
GBS treatment?	PCN G during labor
Women with epilepsy have an increased incidence of what?	Neural tube defects, even if not on antiepileptic medication.
The menstrual cycle consists of two concurrent cycles what are they?	Ovarian and endometrial
What are the two phases of the ovarian cycle?	Follicular days 1-14 and Luteal days 14-28.
LH surge causes what?	Stimulation of ovulation day 14
What causes LH surge?	Estrogen surge
Explain the Follicular phase progression?	FSH stimulates the development of primary ovarian follicle> follicle produces estrogen>estrogen causes uterine lining proliferation > estrogen surge causes LH surge which stimulates the ovulation day 14
When does the Luteal phase begin?	After the ovulation, a remnant of follicle develops into Corpus Luteum
Corpus luteum produces what?	Progesterone to maintain endometrium to receive fertilized ovum.
What are the two phases of Endometrial cycle?	Proliferative days1-14 and Secretory phase days 14-28

Progesterone is dominant in which phase of the Endometrial cycle?	Secretory (Secret progesterone phase)
What happens to the levels of progesterone if there is no fertilization?	It drops
During fertilization, Trophoblast secretes hCG to maintain what?	Corpus Luteum
What is the term used to describe heavy or prolonged bleeding?	Menorrhagia (Know the terms)
What is a term used to describe the cycle which has the length of >35 days?	Oligomenorrhea
What is the term used to describe the cycle which has the length <21 days?	Poly menorrhea
What is the term used to describe the absence of menses for 6 months?	Amenorrhea
What is the term used to describe the cycle which has irregular cycles?	Metrorrhagia - bleeding between regular periods.
Heavy irregular bleeding describes?	Menometrorrhagia
What is the most common cause of dysfunctional uterine bleeding?	Fibroids
Fibroids are most commonly seen in which race?	African American (AA)
Hypomenorrhea is what?	Lack of bleeding - scanty menstruation

Hypomenorrhea is seen with?	Athletes, anorexia, stress, Ashermen's and post myomectomy
What is the most common cause of polymenorrhea?	Anovulation
Patients with Graves and PCOS will have what kind of cycle?	Oligomenorrhea
Lab workup for abnormal bleeding?	CBC, TSH, FSH, PRL, HCG
Diagnostic work-up for abnormal bleeding?	The pelvic US>Endometrial bx>hysteroscopy>D&C
Fibroids have been shown to decrease in the size with the use of?	OCPs
Initial work-up for primary amenorrhea?	Breast/Pelvic exam, Pelvis US, Serum HCG, PRL< FSH, TSH/T4, Testosterone
What's the term used to describe the solid membrane across Introitus?	Imperforate Hymen
What's the term used to describe NO patent vagina?	Vaginal agenesis
What's the treatment for Vaginal agenesis?	Reconstructive surgery
What is the most common cause of secondary amenorrhea?	Pregnancy
In ovarian failure, the labs FSH and LH will be high or low?	High
Hypothalamic failure FSH/LH will be high or low?	Low

What's the treatment for hyperprolactinomas if the patient still desires pregnancy?	If pt is still desiring pregnancy treat by suppressing PRL with Bromocriptine or Cabergoline
Treatment for hyperprolactinomas if pt does not desire pregnancy?	Hormonal contraception
Treatment for unstable bleeding?	IV estrogen
Treatment for PMS?	SSRI
PMS vs Premenstrual dysphoric disorder?	With PMDD you will see functional impairment (missing work etc.)
PMDD treatment for pt not responding to the SSRI or OCPs?	GnRH agonist (Leuprolide acetate)
The average age for menopause?	50-51 years old
What's considered premature menopause?	< 40 years old
Menopause is described as?	Absence of manses for >12 months.
Perimenopausal symptoms are?	Hot flashes sleep issues, mood swings, and vaginal dryness
Hormonal dx of menopause?	FSH>40
What is a Risk for women who have a decrease in estrogen?	Bone loss and CV disease
Risk of starting hormonal therapy several years after the onset of menopause?	MI in 1st 12 months

What is the 2nd most common GYN cancer?	Ovarian
What's significant about ovarian cancer?	It has the highest mortality rate
Which cells are MCC (most common cause) of ovarian malignancy?	Epithelial cell
Risk factors for ovarian cancer?	Nullparity, infertility, age >50, BRCA 1 and 2
What is protective against ovarian cancer?	The use of OCPs
MC (most common) presentation of ovarian cancer?	Ascites
Ovarian cancer METS go to?	Umbilical nodes
Which serum level is used for monitoring the tx of ovarian cancer?	Serum CA-125
What is the useful screening test for the high-risk patient of ovarian cancer?	Transvaginal US
Sister Mary Joseph nodes are seen with which GYN cancer?	Ovarian
MC HPV strands are seen with Cervical cancer?	16, 18, 31, 33 (MC 16 and 18)
Risk factors for cervical cancer?	Early-onset of sex, multiple partners, smoking, CIN and STIs
Cervical cancer is what kind of cancer?	Squamous

Post-coital bleeding/spotting think?	Cervical cancer
Mean age of cervical cancer?	47
What can prevent cervical cancer?	Gardasil vaccine
How is cervical cancer diagnosed?	Colposcopy with bx
A classification system for cervical dysplasia?	Bethesda system
Management of abnormal pap - ASC-US w/negative HPV?	Repeat pap in 12 months
Management of abnormal pap - ASC-US w/positive HPV?	Colposcopy with bx
Management of abnormal pap - LGSIL?	Colposcopy with bx
Management of abnormal pap - HGSIL?	Colposcopy with bx
AGUS work-up?	Colposcopy with cervical and endometrial bx
CIN I vs CIN II and III?	CIN I can be followed w/PAP where CIN II and III need surgical excision
MC non-skin cancer in women?	Breast cancer
MC breast cancer?	Infiltrative DUCTAL carcinoma
Breast cancer presentation?	Painless, hard, fixed lump, any unilateral nipple discharge +/- blood

What's the term used to describe chronic eczematous itchy scaling rash on the nipple and areola?	Paget's
The initial test for breast cancer in females <40 years of age?	US
What kind of bx is done initially?	FNA (fine needle aspiration)
Treatment for breast cancer?	Lumpectomy followed by radiation therapy
When are the Aromatase inhibitors useful in the treatment of breast cancer?	Useful in postmenopausal patients with breast cancer (Letrozole, Anastrozole)
Which anti-estrogen medication is used in tx of breast cancer?	Tamoxifen
Which medication can be used as prevention for breast cancer if pt >35 years old with high risk?	Tamoxifen
MC GYN cancer in the USA?	Endometrial cancer
Endometrial cancer is dependent on which hormone?	Estrogen
Endometrial cancer peak age?	Postmenopausal 50-60 years old
One of the biggest risk factors for Endometrial cancer?	Obesity
Endometrial cancer presentation?	Postmenopausal bleeding

Endometrial cancer dx?	Bx (biopsy) - adenocarcinoma
Endometrial cancer tx (treatment)?	Total hysterectomy w/ bilateral salpingo-oophorectomy, high dose progestin
Vaginal cancer is what type of cancer?	Squamous
Tx for vaginal cancer?	Radiation
Vulvar cancer is what type of cancer?	Squamous
MC location for vulvar cancer?	Labia majora
MC presentation of vulvar cancer?	Pruritus
Vulvar cancer dx?	Red/white ulcerative, crusted lesions, bx
Tx for vulvar cancer?	Surgical excision
What produces progesterone?	Corpus Luteum
The couple has the best chance of conceiving the baby between which days of the menstrual period?	days 7 to 10
Secondary amenorrhea is defined as?	Absence of menses for 3 months in pt with previous menstruations.
Ovulatory dysfunction, androgen excess, hirsutism, obesity, and enlarged ovaries	PCOS

describe what?	
PCOS labs?	**Increased LH, FSH** and decreased estradiol
PCOS dx?	Progesterone challenge test
PCOS tx?	Weight loss, Progesterone, Metformin, Spironolactone
Hyperprolactinoma labs?	Decreased LH/FSH and **increased PRL** get an MRI
Hyperprolactinoma tx?	Transsphenoidal surgery
What's Sheehan's syndrome?	Severe postpartum hemorrhage causing ischemic necrosis of anterior pituitary
PCOS US will show?	A string of pearls or wagon wheel
What's the term that describes painful menses?	Dysmenorrhea
The most common cause of primary dysmenorrhea?	Idiopathic
Primary dysmenorrhea happens due to?	Increased prostaglandins
Dysmenorrhea symptoms?	Normal PE, diffuse pelvic pain with the onset of menses
Dysmenorrhea tx?	NSAIDs
The decrease in what causes the symptoms of menopause?	Estrogen. This will cause the LH/FSH levels to go up

Best tx for a pt with menopause that still has their uterus?	E+P. If no uterus only use estrogen
PMS starts during which phase of the menstrual cycle?	Luteal phase
Which medication can help with symptoms of bloating?	Spironolactone took in the luteal phase
MC bug is seen with Mastitis?	S. Aureus
Mastitis presentation?	Present with unilateral tenderness, heat, significant fever, chills, and other flu-like sx.
Mastitis tx?	Dicloxacillin. Pt is ok to continue with breastfeeding.
Breast abscess tx?	I&D stop breastfeeding from that breast.
MC age group for breast fibroadenoma?	Late teens early 20s
Breast fibroadenoma presentation?	RUBBERY, mobile, well-circumscribed
Breast fibroadenoma tx?	Watchful waiting
MC benign breast disorder?	Fibrocystic disease
Fibrocystic breast presentation?	Tender bilateral, multiple masses, symptoms worst right before menses?
Fibrocystic breast bx will show?	Straw-colored fluid, no blood

Which medication can be given for severe pain with Fibrocystic breast?	Danazol
MCC of GYN visits?	Vaginitis
Vaginitis dx?	Wet-prep
Trichomoniasis is usually transmitted how?	STI
Flagellated protozoan think?	Trichomoniasis
Trichomoniasis signs and symptoms?	Frothy yellow-green discharge, strawberry cervix, dysuria, dyspareunia
Trichomoniasis dx?	Wet-prep (motile trichomonads, movement of flagella)
Trichomoniasis tx?	Single dose of Metronidazole 2 gr
Trichomoniasis pH will be?	>5 usually 6-7
MCC of vaginitis?	BV (Bacterial vaginosis)
Gardnerella vaginalis think?	Bacterial vaginosis
BV symptoms?	The fishy odor that's the worst after sex
BV discharge will be?	Thin white grey fishy smell
BV wet prep will show?	**Clue cells**

BV pH will be?	Between 5 and 6 (BV pH 5-6 and Trich is 6-7)
BV tx?	Metro for 7 days
Atrophic vaginitis is seen in females with?	Decreased estrogen
Atrophic vaginitis presentation?	Pruritus, burning, and dryness
Atrophic vaginitis wet prep will be?	Negative
MC agent in Vaginal Candidiasis	Candida Albicans
Vaginal candidiasis presentation?	White thick clumpy discharge - cottage cheese
Vaginal candidiasis wet prep will show?	Branching hyphae and spores, pH of 4-5
Vaginal candidiasis tx?	Single dose Fluconazole PO
Vaginal candidiasis in the first trimester?	Itraconazole
MC age group for gonorrhea?	20-24 years old
MC sequelae of gonorrhea?	PID
Gonorrhea is what kind of bug?	Gram negative diplococci
Gonorrhea presentation?	Usually asymptomatic, vaginal discharge, increased frequency and dysuria

When testing for gonorrhea also test for?	Chlamydia
Treatment for gonorrhea?	Ceftriaxone 250mg IM
MCC of cervicitis?	Chlamydia
Post-coital bleeding can be a presentation of what?	Chlamydia or cervical cancer
Treatment for Chlamydia?	Azithromycin 1gr PO single dose or Doxy
Painful, grouped vesicles on an erythematous base, think?	Herpes Simplex
Herpes Simplex dx?	Tzanck smear for nucleated giant cells
Herpes Simplex tx?	Acyclovir
The term used for genital warts?	Condyloma - cauliflower appearance
Condyloma acuminata is caused by?	HPV 6 and 11
What is the most common treatment for Condyloma acuminata?	Cryotherapy
MCC of PID?	N. Gonorrhea
What is PID (Pelvic Inflammatory Disease)?	Ascending infection of the upper reproductive tract
MC serious complication of STD?	PID

PID presentation?	Pelvic/lower abdominal pain, dysuria, dyspareunia, vaginal discharge, N/V, fever
PID PE will show?	+ Chandelier sign= cervical motion tenderness
PID treatment?	Ceftriaxone IM (gon/chlam) + doxycycline
Syphilis is what?	Spirochete sexually transmitted, Treponemal pallidum
Syphilis presentation?	Painless, red, raised, firm ulcer >1cm - **CHANCRE**
Syphilis diagnosis?	VDRL and RPR
Syphilis tx?	PCN G, follow the RPR and VDRL titers
Chancroid is hard to dx because of difficulty isolating what in the lab?	Haemophilus ducreyi (think HD-Chancroid)
Chancroid presentation?	Painful Genital ulcers have an erythematous base; the borders are clearly demarcated and the ulcer is usually covered with a gray or yellow purulent exudate and bleeds when scraped.
Chancroid vs Chancre?	Chancre (syphilis) is **painless**! (easiest way to tell them apart)
Chancroid tx?	Azithromycin 1gr PO single dose or Ceftriaxone 250mg IM
Lymphogranuloma venereum is a genital ulcer disease caused by?	L1, L2, and L3 serovars of *Chlamydia trachomatis*

Diagnosis of LGV?	Men who have sex with men (MSM) who present with proctitis, enlarged inguinal lymph nodes, and the presence of anorectal ulcers
LGV tx?	Doxycycline 100 mg orally twice daily for **21 days**
Most commonly pelvic organ prolapse happens at what age?	After the menopause >50.
What's a cystocele?	Bladder prolapse (posterior bladder herniation into the anterior vagina)
Pelvic organ prolapse will show what on the exam?	Bulging mass that increases with Valsalva
Pelvic organ prolapse treatment?	Kegels, pessaries, surgery (surgery only if symptomatic)
Cystocele physical exam findings will be?	Visualization of downward movement of the anterior vaginal wall with Valsalva.
What is uterine prolapse?	Uterine herniation into the vagina
What is a rectocele?	Distal sigmoid colon into the posterior vagina
Rectocele can happen due to the damage?	Rectovaginal septum
Rectocele physical exam findings?	Visualization of upward movement of the posterior vaginal wall with Valsalva
Ovarian torsion is what?	Complete or partial rotation of the ovary on its ligamentous supports.

MC initial imaging that's done for ovarian torsion?	The pelvic US
Ovarian torsion treatment?	Surgery ASAP
Patch-Ortho Evra is less effective in pt that?	Weight >200lb
Side effects of Progestin-only OCPs?	Irregular bleeding
Depo Provera is what kind of contraceptive?	Progestin-only
Depo Provera side effects?	Weight gain, irregular bleeding, amenorrhea, delay in the **return of ovulation for 1.5 years**
The presence of normal endometrial tissue outside of the endometrial cavity is?	Endometriosis
MC site of Endometriosis?	Ovaries
MC cause of Endometriosis?	Infertility
Classic presenting triad of Endometriosis?	**CYCLIC** premenstrual pelvic pain, dysmenorrhea, dyspareunia
Endometriosis dx?	Laparoscopy w bx
Chocolate cyst think?	Endometrioma
Endometriosis tx?	OCPs, NSAIDs, Danazol is also a great choice

Powder burn and Mulberry lesions, think?	Endometriosis
Most ovarian cysts are what type?	Functional
Ovarian cyst dx?	The pelvic US
What size ovarian cysts need surgery?	>8cm
A complication of ovarian cysts?	Ovarian torsion
What is another term for Leiomyoma?	Fibroids
What are fibroids?	They are benign smooth muscle tumors
Fibroid production is related to?	Estrogen production
Fibroids usually regress when?	Regress with menopause
MC presentation of fibroids?	Bleeding
Fibroids are diagnosed with?	The pelvic US
What is a surgical treatment of fibroids to preserve fertility?	Myomectomy
Definitive tx for fibroids?	Hysterectomy
MC reason for the hysterectomy is?	Fibroids

What is stress incontinence?	Urine leakage due to increased intra-abdominal pressure
Urine leakage from sneezing or laughing?	Stress incontinence
Stress incontinence tx?	Kegels/Pelvic floor exercises
Overactive bladder aka?	Urge incontinence
Urge incontinence is due to?	Detrusor muscle overactivity
Urge incontinence tx?	Bladder training, Detrol or Oxybutynin
The underactive bladder will cause what kind of incontinence?	Overflow incontinence
Overflow incontinence other causes?	BPH, strictures
Overflow incontinence presentation?	Increased post-void residual >200mL, dribbling
How's infertility described?	Failure to conceive with 1 year of regular unprotected sex
MCC of infertility in females?	Occulted fallopian tubes and ovulatory factors such as PCOS
Infertility in females what is an initial diagnostic test?	Hysterosalpingography
Infertility in females' medication treatment?	Clomid- Clomiphene
Hysterosalpingography will show what in case of infertility?	Adhesions

Fetal heart tones monitoring starts when?	At the 10 weeks
What's a Ladin sign?	Uterus softening at 6 weeks
What's Hegar's sign?	Uterine isthmus shortening at 6-8 weeks
What's Goodell's sign?	Cervix softening 4-5 weeks
What's Chadwick's sign?	Cervix and vulva bluish color at 8-10 weeks
Quickening occurs when?	At 16 weeks
How do we estimate the date of delivery?	1st day of LMP + 7 days - 3 months (If the first day of LMP was April 10, Next add 7 days= April 17, now minus 3 months = January 17 is expected date of delivery) **(This is a kind of question you might be pimped on during the clinical year in your OB rotation)**
When is glucose tolerance tested?	At 24-28 weeks
When is Rhogam given?	At 28 weeks and within 72 hours of delivery if mom is Rh-
If the mother is Rh- will the firstborn baby be affected?	The firstborn child will not be affected
When do we test for GBS during the pregnancy?	32-37 weeks

When is amniocentesis done?	15-18 weeks
How's GBS treated in pregnancy?	PCN during labor
Biophysical profile BPP consists of 5 parameters what are they?	NST, Amniotic fluid level, gross fetal movements, fetal tone, and fetal breathing
When does the N/V begin in pregnancy?	Usually, the onset is at 5-6 weeks, peak at 9, usually resolve at 16
What is the severe form of N/V during pregnancy called?	Hyperemesis gravidarum - admit this pt
When is the cystic fibrosis screening done?	At 10-13 weeks
How is the cystic fibrosis screening done?	Nuchal translucency with the US
When is the QUAD screen done?	At 15-22 weeks, try around 16 weeks for best results
What is the QUAD screen?	AFP, hCG, Estriol, inhibin A
1st trimester has the best detection for?	Downs
The second trimester detects?	Neural Tube Defects (NTD)
Pregnancy CV (cardiovascular) effects?	Decrease SVR and arterial BP
Pregnancy Heme effects?	Increase in plasma volume and decreased hematocrit
How does the pregnancy affect the GFR?	GFR will go up during the pregnancy

How's the rupture of the membrane diagnosed?	Ferning under a microscope, Nitrazine positive on pH paper, the pool of fluid in the vagina
What's stage 1 of labor?	The onset of labor to full dilation of the cervix (10cm)
What's stage 2 of labor?	Cervix dilation until end of delivery of the neonate
What's stage 3 of labor?	Postpartum until end of delivery of the placenta
What's stage 4 of labor?	Period 2 hours after delivery
What is the Braxton-Hicks contraction?	Spontaneous uterine contractions late in pregnancy not associated with cervical dilation
What's effacement?	Cervical softening and thinning out, expressed in %.
What's the station?	Location of presenting part in relation to maternal ischial spines
Accelerations of an increase of 15bpm for 15 sec in considered?	Normal baby
With the early decelerations think?	Head compression
Variable decelerations think?	Cord compression
Late decelerations think?	Uteroplacental insufficiency
When delivering the baby which shoulder part should be delivered first?	Anterior

What is the major risk of vaginal delivery after prior c-section?	Uterine rupture
Where is the Pudendal block given?	Behind ischial spine at the sacrospinous ligament
MC location for an epidural?	L3-L4 interspace
What is the risk of giving the epidural?	Maternal HYPOtension
MC presentation of infants during birth?	Vertex - head down
MC presentation of twins?	Vertex-vertex
Delivery of triplets has to be done via?	C-section
What is considered a normal APGAR score?	Score >7
MCC of abortions?	Fetal chromosomal abnormalities
MCC of 1st trimester bleeding?	Threatened Abortion
Threatened abortion is?	Cervical os is closed, bleeding, No POC, the baby is ok
Threatened abortion tx?	Supportive
What's missed abortion?	Cervical Os is closed, no POC expelled but the embryo is not viable
Missed abortion tx in 1st trimester?	D&C

Missed abortion tx after 1st trimester?	D&E
What's complete abortion?	Cervical Os closed, all POC expelled
What's inevitable abortion?	Progressive cervix dilation, No POC expelled
What's tx for inevitable abortion?	D&E if 2nd trimester and Rhogam if indicated
What's the incomplete abortion?	Dilated cervix, some POC expelled some still in the uterus
Which medication is used to induce labor?	Pitocin
What's Placenta abruption?	Premature separation of the placenta
MCC of placenta abruption?	HTN
MC placental abruptions happen when?	Before labor
Placental abruption presentation?	Sever abd PAIN with bleeding and contractions
Placental abruption dx?	Pelvic US (DON'T do a pelvic exam)
Placental abruption tx?	Delivery of fetus
What's Placenta previa?	Abnormal implantation of placenta over cervical os
Placenta previa vs abruption?	Previa is PAINLESS

MC risk factor for Placenta previa?	Prior C-section
MC complication of placenta previa?	Accreta
What's Accreta?	Abnormal growth of placenta through the myometrium
Placenta previa presentation?	PAINLESS bleeding in the 3rd trimester, bright red
PE for placenta previa?	The digital cervix exam is Contraindicated.
Placenta previa dx?	US
Placenta previa tx?	Pelvic rest, bed rest, admit
MCC of maternal deaths?	Ectopic pregnancy
MC location of ectopic pregnancy?	Fallopian tube
MC risk factors for ectopic pregnancy?	Prior ectopic, PID, hx of tubal ligation
Ectopic pregnancy presentation?	Unilateral pelvic/abd pain, vaginal bleeding, amenorrhea
Ectopic pregnancy pelvic exam will show?	Cervical motion tenderness, adnexal mass
Ectopic pregnancy dx?	Serial quantitative B-hCG. It will fail to double in ectopic within 24-48 hours (Normal pregnancy the B-hCG will double within 24-48 hr). Also, get Transvaginal US

Ectopic pregnancy - transvaginal US will show?	Absence of gestational sac
Ectopic pregnancy medication tx?	Methotrexate
Ectopic pregnancy tx if a suspected rupture in stable pt?	Laparoscopy, Laparotomy if unstable
Treatment of choice for a stable pt with ectopic pregnancy who has hCG<5000 and tubal size <4cm?	Methotrexate IM
Gestational diabetes is caused by?	It's caused by the placental release of human placental lactogen (HPL) which antagonizes insulin
Screening test for Gestational diabetes?	50gr oral glucose challenge test nonfasting at 24-28 weeks. If >140 in 1hr preform 3h oral GTT.
3-hour GTT test is positive if?	Pt meets 2 of the 3. 1hr>180, 2h>155, 3h>140
Diabetes treatment of choice in pregnancy?	Insulin
Patients with gestational diabetes should be rescreened when after the delivery?	6 weeks after the delivery
Gestational HTN should resolve by?	12 weeks postpartum
Gestational HTN may develop into?	Preeclampsia
Gestational HTN dx?	Increased BP with No proteinuria

Triad of preeclampsia?	HTN + proteinuria + edema after 20 weeks
What's considered mild HTN?	>140/90
What's considered severe HTN?	>160/110, Proteinuria >5g/24h
What's HELLP syndrome?	**H**emolytic Anemia, **E**levated **L**iver Enzymes, **L**ow **P**latelets
What medication is given to help with fetal lung development?	Betamethasone at 26-30 weeks
Mild HTN tx?	Delivery is only cure
Severe HTN tx?	Delivery is only cure
Severe HTN medication tx?	Hydralazine or Labetalol, give Mg Sulfate as well to prevent eclampsia
Treatment for seizure in pregnancy?	Mg Sulfate
Abnormal labor progression is termed?	Dystocia
MC indication for c-section?	Dystocia
Increase pelvic opening with hyperflexion of hips describes which maneuver?	McRobert's maneuver
Premature rupture of membranes is before what week?	Before 37

What's the prolapsed umbilical cord?	The cord is delivered before the baby
Prolapsed umbilical cord tx?	Quick delivery via c-section
MCC of perinatal mortality?	Pre-term labor
What can be given to the patient to suppress uterine contractions?	Tocolytics (Terbutaline, Mg Sulfate)
MCC of postpartum hemorrhage?	Uterine atony
What's Uterine atony?	Soft, boggy uterus with dilated cervix
Uterine atony tx?	Oxytocin IV, Misopristol
MCC of endometritis?	GABHS and S. Aureus
Endometritis MC presents when?	2-3 days postpartum with fever

Good luck on your test! You have studied hard and I'm sure you will do just fine, remember "Thousand's and thousand's of students done this before you, so can you PERIOD". **PLEASE DO ME A HUGE FAVOR AND LEAVE AN AMAZON COMMENT FOR THE BOOK. THAT HELPS ME A LOT AND LET'S OTHER STUDENTS KNOW IF YOU FOUND THIS BOOK HELPFUL. THANK YOU!!!!!!**

Pediatrics

The most common cause of death in physical abuse?	Head injury
MC (most common) sinus involved with orbital sinusitis?	Ethmoid
Medication treatment used for bedwetting?	Desmopressin (DDAVP)
MC cause of diarrhea in children?	Rotavirus
Kawasaki disease is most common in what population?	Asians <5 years old (Kawasaki is made in Asia)
When does the newborn cord typically come out?	1 week to 10 days
Strabismus should resolve by what age?	4 months if not get an optho referral
What's normal newborn feeding intake?	100cc/kilo/day
Strep pharyngitis should always be treated for how long?	10 days to prevent rheumatic fever
Treatment of choice for strep pharyngitis?	PCN VK
When can patients with strep return to the school?	After being on ABX for 24hr.
Otitis Media (OM) treatment?	Amoxicillin 90mg/kg/day divided into 2 doses x 10 days
MC bug causing Otitis media?	S. Pneumonia
What is an OM treatment if a patient has a PCN allergy?	Ceftriaxone, **Cefdinir**

What's considered recurrent OM?	3+ episodes of AOM in 6 months or 4+ in one year
Perforated tympanic membrane due to infection treatment is?	Amoxicillin + Ofloxacin drops
If amoxicillin fails the next step in management for OM is?	Augmentin
MC bug causing the Otitis Externa?	Pseudomonas
Itchy eyes are most likely?	Allergic conjunctivitis
Why should we treat peds conjunctivitis?	50% is bacterial so treat even if suspected viral
Treatment for peds conjunctivitis?	Ocuflox drops 1 drop QID till clear for 2 days
MC cause of croup?	Parainfluenza virus
The child presents with a barking cough, think?	Croup
Samter's triad is?	Aspirin sensitivity, nasal polyposis, and asthma
What is a drug of choice (DOC) for pertussis?	Macrolide (Azithromycin)
What are the chances that the baby will be getting an HSV-2 from mom during the delivery?	50%
Eczema herpeticum treatment?	IV Acyclovir

Criteria for acute rheumatic fever?	Jones
To suspect Kawasaki disease fever should be present for at least how many days?	5 days
A most serious complication of Kawasaki disease?	Coronary artery aneurysm
Kawasaki treatment?	IVIG and aspirin
Genetic cardiomyopathy caused by mutation of the cardiac sarcomere?	Hypertrophic Cardiomyopathy aka HOCM (this is the condition when you hear a young athlete dropped dead on the field from the heart problem)
HOCM is characterized by?	Left ventricular hypertrophy
HOCM inheritance pattern?	**A**utosomal dominant (HOCM drives **A** dominant auto)
Patients with HOCM are at increased risk for what?	Sudden cardiac death
MC cancer amongst the 15-19 years-old patients?	Hodgkin's lymphoma
Reed Sterling Cells should make you think of what?	Hodgkin's lymphoma (Have you REED about Hodgkin's)
Lymphoblast should make you think of?	ALL
Auer rods should make you think of?	AML
Myeloblasts should make you think of?	AML (M from AML for Myeloblasts)

Persistent acne and hirsutism are a red flag for what?	Hyperandrogenism (PCOS, tumors)
Inflammation of pilosebaceous units?	Acne vulgaris
The itch that rashes, think?	Atopic Dermatitis
What's the allergic triad?	Eczema, allergic rhinitis, asthma
MC location for eczema in infants?	Face and extensor surfaces
MC location of eczema in adults?	Flexor surfaces
Tapioca pudding vesicles, think?	Dyshidrotic dermatitis
Dyshidrotic dermatitis treatment?	Topical steroid ointment, cold compresses
Oval **coin-shaped** weeping patches?	**Nummular** dermatitis
Harold patch should make you think?	Pityriasis Rosea
Pityriasis Rosea will have what pattern of distribution?	**Christmas tree pattern**
Pityriasis Rosea lesions description?	**Salmon-colored** oval/round papules with white circular scaling, very pruritis
Pityriasis Rosea treatment?	None needed its self resolving
What is Darier's sign?	Localized urticaria appearing where the skin is rubbed

Target lesions should make you think of?	Erythema Multiforme (**Target the erythema with multiform**)
Erythema Multiforme lesion description?	Dusty violet/red, purpuric macule/vesicle, or bullae in the center, surrounded by a pale edematous rim and peripheral red halo.
Erythema Multiforme treatment?	Stop the offending drug, antihistamines, skincare
MC meds causing the SJS and TEN?	**Sulfa** and anticonvulsant drugs
SJS vs TEN percentage of skin involved?	TEN is >30% and SJS is <10% (**TEN is 30+**)
MC bug causing the Impetigo?	S. Aureus
Impetigo buzzword?	**Honey-colored crusted**
Impetigo treatment?	Bactroban 2% ointment if extensive Keflex
MC (most common) cause of Molluscum Contagiosum?	Viral (**poxviridae family**)
Molluscum Contagiosum buzzword?	**Dome-shaped**, flesh-colored, **central umbilication**
Lice treatment?	Permethrin 1% shampoo, wash clothing and bedding (**Lice and scabies should get PERMIT lice 1% and scabies 5%**)
Scabies buzzword?	Linear burrows

Scabies treatment?	**Permethrin 5% cream** from the neck down wash it off after 8-14hr, repeat in one week.
HPV 6&11 should make you think of?	Condyloma accuminata (genital warts)
Common warts aka?	**Verruca** Vulgaris
Parkland formula is used for what?	Burns
What is the Parkland formula?	LR @ 4ml x kg x BSA burn (1/2 given in 1st 8 hr, rest over next 16 hr.)
Only childhood viral exanthem that starts on the trunk and spread to the face?	Roseola 6th disease (**Imagine rose on the trunk, smell of the rose goes up**)
MC virus causing Hand-Foot-Mouth Dz?	**Coxsackie** A virus
Which virus causes mumps?	**Paramyxovirus**
MC complications of mumps?	**Orchitis**, pancreatitis, can cause deafness
3 Cs of measles/rubeola?	Cough, Corzy, conjunctivitis
Measles rash starts where?	At the **hairline spreading down**, fever is concurrent with a rash
MC complication of measles?	OM, encephalitis
How long does the measles rash last?	7 days

How long does German measles rash last?	3 days
MC virus that causes Rubella/German measles?	Togavirus
Erythema Infectiosum (5th disease) is caused by which virus?	**Parvovirus B19** (remember **5B19**)
Erythema Infectiosum buzzwords?	**Slapped cheek**, lacy reticular rash on extremities (spares palms and soles)
Describe the neonatal jaundice timeframes?	**Physiological** is first it occurs in the **first 3-5 days. Breastfeeding** jaundice next occurs in the **first week** of life. **Breast milk jaundice occurs in the second week of life**.
Perioral dermatitis is MC seen in which patient population?	Young woman
This rash **spares vermillion border**?	Perioral dermatitis
Perioral dermatitis treatment?	Topical **Metro**nidazole or Erythromycin
Inflammation of one or both corners of the mouth?	Angular cheilitis
Diaper dermatitis treatment?	Barrier creams, air drying or mild steroid
Erythematous rash with **distinct satellite lesions**, think?	Yeast Diaper candida
Yeasts Diaper candida treatment?	Clotrimazole ointment

Atopic dermatitis is likely a dysfunction of which protein in the epidermis?	Filaggrin protein
Eczema treatment?	High strength topical steroids and antihistamine for itching
Cradle cap aka?	Seborrheic dermatitis
Seborrheic dermatitis treatment?	Selenium sulfide, Ketoconazole (shampoo or cream)
Pityriasis Rosea can mimic what other diseases?	Syphilis so do PRP if the pt is sexually active
Is SJS more common in children or adults?	Children (TEN in adults)
What stimulates sebum production?	Androgens
Scabies is what type of hypersensitivity reaction?	Type 4
Small red spots in buccal mucosa with blue/white pale centers, think?	Koplik spots
Measles rash lasts how many days?	7 days
Forchheimer's spots on the soft palate, think?	Rubella
Lymphadenopathy is associated with which viral exanthem?	Rubella/German measles
Sickle cell patients can get aplastic crisis from which exanthem?	5th slapped cheeks

Herpes Zoster/shingles are most contagious when?	The day before the rash appears
Dewdrop on a rose petal, think?	Vericella
MC sites of zoster eruption?	Thoracic and lumbar
Zoster infection pattern?	Dermatomal
Varicella rash starts where?	At the hairline and spreads down
Bells palsy is associated with witch HSV?	HSV1
MC cause of encephalitis?	HSV
HSV is diagnosed with which smear?	Tzanck smear
Most sensitive test for Varicella-zoster?	PCR
Shingles treatment?	Acyclovir, Valacyclovir
Most painful type of all burns?	Superficial partial-thickness
Painful burn with blisters?	Superficial partial-thickness
Painful burn without the blisters?	Superficial burn
Burn with blisters but no pain?	Deep partial-thickness

Burn that's waxy white?	Full-thickness
Burn treatment of fingers and toes?	They should be wrapped individually to prevent maceration
MC used abx for 2nd and 3rd-degree burns?	Silver sulfadiazine
Name the second-degree burns?	Superficial partial and deep partial (Dermis involved)
Treatment for onychomycosis (fungal nail infection)?	Terbinafine
Treatment for tinea capitus?	Griseofulvin
Ringworm aka?	Tinea corporis
Weber test will localize to?	To the affected ear
Bone conduction over air conduction is seen with?	Abnormal Rinne test
MC cause of conductive hearing loss?	OM, serous otitis and cerumen impaction
MC cause of sensorineural hearing loss?	Noise exposure, drugs, and aging
MC bugs causing bacterial conjunctivitis?	Staph/strep
Will bacterial conjunctivitis cause vision issues?	Usually no vision changes
Bacterial conjunctivitis will present with what?	Purulent discharge glued shut on awakening, absence of ciliary injection

What bug should we think about covering in contact wearers?	Pseudomonas
MC population affected by Orbital cellulitis?	Children
How to tell pre-septal cellulitis vs orbital cellulitis?	Pain with ocular movement and decreased vision will be present with orbital cellulitis
How to diagnose orbital cellulitis?	High res CT
Orbital cellulitis treatment?	IV ABX (Vanco, Clinda)
Otitis media is MC preceded by?	URI
Treatment for recurrent or persistent OM?	Tympanostomy
If intranasal decongestants are used >5 days this can cause?	Rhinitis medicamentosa
Treatment for allergic rhinitis?	Intranasal glucocorticoids (fluticasone)
Nasal polyps can be seen in kids with?	Cystic Fibrosis
MC cause of Mastoiditis?	Prolonged or inadequately treated Acute Otitis Media
Mastoiditis treatment?	IV ABX and myringotomy
MC location of epistaxis?	Anterior - Kiesselbach's plexus
MC cause of epistaxis in children?	Fingernails trauma

What kind of epistaxis should be referred to ENT?	Posterior bleed
MC artery involved in posterior epistaxis?	Sphenopalatine artery
Centor criteria for pharyngitis is?	Fever, tender anterior cervical adenopathy, lack of cough and pharyngotonsilar exudate
Strep pharyngitis treatment?	PCN VK 10 days
Which vaccine can help prevent epiglottis?	Hib
Think epiglottitis if a child presents with?	Drooling, sitting in the sniffing tripod position leaning forward
MC cause of epiglottitis?	Hib
3 Ds of Epiglottitis?	Dysphagia, drooling and distress
Inspiratory stridor think?	Epiglottitis
Epiglottitis diagnostic test?	Lateral neck x-ray showing the **Thumbprint sign**
The child with epiglottitis in severe distress should go to?	OR to establish a surgical airway
Steeple sign on x-ray, think?	Croup
MC bug causing Peritonsillar abscess?	Strep pyogenes
Deviation of the uvula on the exam, think?	Peritonsillar abscess

Muffled hot potato voice, think?	Peritonsillar abscess
Peritonsillar abscess treatment?	Drainage and ABX (Amoxicillin)
What is strabismus?	Misalignment of the eyes.
Screening test for strabismus?	Hirschberg corneal light reflex test
Cover-uncover test is used for?	To determine the angle of strabismus
Conservative therapy for strabismus?	Patch therapy cover the good eye
If strabismus is not corrected by age 2 what can develop?	Amblyopia
Radial head subluxation, think?	Nursemaids elbow
What ligament is involved in Nursemaids' elbow?	Annular ligament
Nursemaids elbow treatment?	Reduction
MC age group for slipped Capital Femoral Epiphysis(SCFE)?	7 to 16 years-old
How will leg be rotated in SCFE?	External rotation
Xray of SCFE will show?	Ice cream slipping off a cone
X-ray of SCFE will show which displacement?	Posterior and inferior

If the question talks about an obese adolescent with knee pain and limp think?	SCFE
SCFE pt will have what range of motion decreased?	Internal rotation and abduction
SCFE treatment?	ORIF
MC cause of chronic knee pain in young active adolescents?	Osgood-Schllaters Disease
Osgood-Schllaters Disease is located where?	Anterior tibial tuberosity
Osgood-Schllaters Disease treatment?	RICE, NSAIDs, quadriceps stretching
MC age group of scoliosis?	8 to 10, MC in girls
Scoliosis is dx if what angle is >10 degrees?	Cobbs angle measured on AP/Lat films
Most sensitive test for scoliosis?	Adams forward bending test
When is the surgical correction needed for scoliosis?	If cobbs angle is >40 degrees
Congenital hip dysplasia is seen with?	Firstborn girls
Which babies should get an ultrasound test for suspected congenital hip dysplasia?	All females breech babies
Physical exam tests for congenital hip dysplasia?	Barlow and Ortolani

Treatment for congenital hip dysplasia in kids <6 months of age?	Pavlik harness for 6 weeks
Avascular necrosis of proximal femur?	Leg-Calve-Perthes disease
MC age group for Leg-Calve-Perthes disease?	4 to 10 (SCFE is usually over 10)
MC benign bone tumor in children?	Osteochondroma
Osteochondroma MC presentation?	Painless mass
Osteochondroma MC location?	Metaphyseal region of the long bones
MC location for enchondroma?	Hands
Bone pain w/o constitutional symptoms?	Osteosarcoma
MC malignant bone tumor?	Osteosarcoma
Osteosarcoma MC location?	Metaphyseal region of the long bones
Osteosarcoma MC METS go to?	Lungs
Osteosarcoma x-ray will show?	Sunray burst
Ewing Sarcoma x-ray will show?	Onion skin
MC Juvenile rheumatoid arthritis?	Pauci-articular

Pauci-articular MC involves which joints?	Large joints
Fixed split S2, think?	Atrial septal defect
MC cause of Atrial septal defect?	Ostium secundum
Atrial septal defect location?	Systolic ejection murmur at the pulmonary area LUSB
Atrial septal defect ECHO will show?	The dilated right atrium and right ventricle
MC type of congenital heart disease?	VSD Ventricular Septal Defect
VSD is heard best where?	LLSB, loud high-pitched harsh, holosystolic murmur
Increased BP upper>lower extremities?	Coarctation of the aorta
Coarctation of the aorta is what kind of murmur?	The systolic murmur that radiates to the back/scapula
Coarctation of the aorta is associated with which syndromes?	Turners and Shones
Coarctation of the aorta diagnostic test?	Angiogram
Coarctation of the aorta x-ray will show?	Rib notching, a figure of 3
Machine-like murmur, think?	Patent Ductus Arteriosus (PDA)
Patent Ductus Arteriosus (PDA) diagnostic test?	ECHO

Patent Ductus Arteriosus (PDA) treatment?	IV Indomethacin
MC cyanotic congenital heart disease?	TOF - Tetralogy of Fallot (kid turns blue)
TOF x-ray will show?	Boot-shaped heart
Eisenmenger's syndrome is seen with?	PDA, VSD, and TOF
TOF is what kind of murmur?	Harsh holosystolic murmur heard best at LUSB
MC involved a valve with rheumatic fever?	Mitral
HOCM MC initial complaint?	Dyspnea
HOCM intensity increases with?	Valsalva and standing
HOCM is best heard where?	LUSB Harsh systolic crescendo-decrescendo murmur
HOCM intensity decreases with?	Finger squeeze or squatting
HOCM ECHO will show?	Asymmetric wall thickness (septal)
1st line meds for HOCM?	Beta-blockers
A serious cause of syncope in children?	Congenital long QT syndrome
Congenital long QT syndrome is what QT interval?	>440 milliseconds

Congenital long QT syndrome treatment?	Beta-blockers
Whats orthostatic hypotension?	Drop-in systolic BP by 20 or diastolic BP of at least 10
MC cause of Acute Bronchiolitis?	RSV
MC age group affected by RSV?	<2yo
MC cause of croup?	Parainfluenza virus
Barking cough think?	Croup
Croup X-ray sign?	Steeple sign
Croup treatment?	Cool humidified air, Single dose of Dexamethasone IM
When should the nebulized epinephrine be used in the treatment of croup?	Severe cases
MC cause of neonatal pneumonia?	Group B strep
MC cause of lower respiratory tract infection?	RSV
MC chronic disease in childhood?	Asthma
Asthma symptoms triad?	Wheezing, dyspnea, and cough
Will asthma have hyper or hyporesonance?	Hyperresonance

Best way to assess the severity of asthma and patient response in the ER?	Peak Expiratory Flow Rate (PEFR)
What PEFR % indicates a good response to the treatment?	>15%
What pulse ox reading is indicative of respiratory distress?	<90%
The gold standard to dx asthma?	PFT
ABG is asthma exacerbation?	Respiratory alkalosis
Examples of systemic corticosteroids?	Prednisone, Methylprednisone, Prednisolone
Examples of inhaled corticosteroids?	Beclomethasone, Flunisolide, Triamcinolone (DOC for a long term, persistent asthma)
DOC (drug of choice) for severe uncontrolled asthma?	Omalizumab
TOC (treatment of choice) for asthmatics with allergic rhinitis?	Leukotriene modifiers (Montelukast)
Treatment for intermittent asthma?	Step 1 (SABA - Albuterol)
Treatment for mild persistent asthma?	step 2 low dose ICS (Fluticasone)
Aspiration dx and treatment of choice?	Bronchoscopy
Hyaline membrane disease aka?	RDS respiratory distress syndrome

RDS is caused by what?	Pulmonary surfactant deficiency
MC respiratory disease of premature infants?	RDS
Sx of RDS?	Decreased breath sounds with crackles
RDS cxr will show?	Diffuse bilateral atelectasis (ground glass appearance) and diaphragm doming
Cystic fibrosis has what type of inheritance?	Autosomal recessive
You should suspect cystic fibrosis if the full-term infant presents with what?	Meconium ileus
Pt with CF will have what kind of stool?	Bulky pale/foul-smelling stool
MC infecting bug in pt with CF?	Pseudomonas
DX od CF?	Sweat chloride test >60mmoi/L
MC cause of Bronchiectasis in the USA?	CF
5 examples of obstructive lung disorders?	Asthma, COPD, Bronchiectasis, CF and Coal workers pneumoconiosis
MC virus causing Gastroenteritis?	Rotavirus for kids and Norovirus for adults
What cap refill is indicative of dehydration?	>3sec

MC cause of appendicitis?	Fecalith
Where does the appendicitis pain first begin?	Periumbilical
What is a Rovsing sign?	RLQ pain with LLQ palpation
Appendicitis CBC will show?	Leukocytosis
MC cause of intestinal obstruction in infancy?	Pyloric stenosis
Use of what medication can increase the incidence of pyloric stenosis?	Erythromycin
Buzzwords for pyloric stenosis?	NON-bilious vomiting, projectile vomiting, olive-shaped mass
Test of choice for pyloric stenosis?	US
Intussusception MC occurs where?	Ileocolic junction
Intussusception buzzword?	Currant jelly stool, sausage-shaped mass
Intussusception test of choice?	Barium contrast enema
Hirschsprung disease is the absence of what cells?	Enteric ganglion cells
MC cause of encopresis?	Constipation
Which hepatitis is the only one that causes spiking fever?	Hep A

When do we worry about jaundice?	Within the first 24 hours of life
Double bubble appearance on x-ray?	Duodenal atresia
Which hernia can appear at birth?	Umbilical
What's hiatal hernia?	Protrusion of the stomach through the diaphragm via the esophageal hiatus
Indirect Hernia passage?	Triple I (Internal, inguinal ring, inguinal canal)
Direct Inguinal hernia?	External canal, Hesselbach triangle
Diagnostic test for lactose intolerance?	Lactose breath hydrogen test
Meckels diverticulum test?	99m technetium pertechnetate/Meckel's scan
Pinworm parasite?	Enterobius vermicularis
MC parasitic intestinal infection?	Pinworms
Pinworm test?	Cellophane tape test
Pinworm treatment?	Albendazole
Posterior cervical lymphadenopathy, think?	EBV (MONO)
Mono patients should avoid doing what?	Contact sports for 1 month

Mono test?	Heterophile antibody test
Influenza is characterized by which symptoms?	ABRUPT onset of fever, HA, chills, malaise
Oral medication for the treatment of flu with/in the first 48h of unset?	Oseltamivir
Severe coughing fits are seen with which phase of pertussis?	Paroxysmal phase
Coxsackievirus A16 causes?	Hand-foot-mouth disease
MC cause of acute pancreatitis in children?	Mumps
Pincer grasp develops when?	At 10 months
Babies start to roll over when?	At 4 months
Stranger anxiety starts at?	9 months
Babies can transfer objects from hand to hand when?	At 6 months
When do babies regain their birth weight at?	At 2 weeks
When does the baby's weight double?	At 4 months
A newborn baby should get what vaccine?	Hep B
The flu vaccine can be given when?	At 6 months

MC type of seizure in infancy?	Febrile
A febrile seizure is what kind of seizure?	Tonic-clonic
Duration of the simple febrile seizures?	<15 min
Febrile seizure treatment?	Lorazepam if >5 min
Staring spells?	Absence seizure (Petit mal)
How do we evaluate the seizure?	EEG
How long is the seizure treated?	Until seizure free for 1-2 years
What is a prewarning for the tonic-clonic seizure?	Auras
MC seizure type?	Complex Partial
Tx for absence seizure?	Ethosuximide or Valproic acid
Valproic acid aka?	Depakote
Levetiracetam aka?	Keppra
What's the WEST syndrome?	Triad of infantile spasms, developmental regression, and hypsarrhythmia
MC causes of bacterial meningitis in neonates?	Group B Strep, E. coli, and Listeria

MC causes of bacterial meningitis in children 1m to 18 years old?	N. meningitis
Bacterial meningitis treatment for neonates?	Ampicillin
Bacterial meningitis treatment for 1m-18y?	Ceftriaxone and Vanco
What's Kernig sign?	Inability to straighten knee with hip flexion
What's Brudzinski sign?	Neck flexion produces knee/hip flexion
What could be the only sign of meningitis in infants?	fever
Bacterial meningitis cells count will be?	>2000, neutrophils 100-10000 PMN
Bacterial meningitis CSF?	Increased WBC, Increased Protein and decreased glucose
45XO is what?	Turner's syndrome
Hallmarks of Turner's syndrome?	Webbed neck, low hairline, hypogonadism
Low set small ears and protruding tongue?	Down's syndrome
MC type of child maltreatment in the USA?	Neglect
To diagnose ADHD symptoms must be present before what age?	Age 7
Autism screening tool?	M-CHAT done at 18 months

Refusal to maintain minimally normal body weight is called what?	Anorexia Nervosa
Anorexia Nervosa is dx under what BMI?	<17.5
Teeth pitting or enamel erosion think?	Bulimia Nervosa
Anorexia Nervosa vs Bulimia Nervosa?	Bulimia Nervosa patients have normal weight or overweight
Bulimia Nervosa treatment?	CBT
MC preventable cause of intellectual disability?	Fetal Alcohol syndrome
Cause of physiologic anemia?	Decrease in erythropoiesis
MC cause of microcytic anemia?	Iron deficiency
MC cause of macrocytic anemia?	B12 and folate deficiency
Purely breastfed infants are at increased risk for what?	Iron deficiency
Sickle cell disease has what inheritance pattern?	Autosomal recessive (sickle cell kids love recess and auto- cars)
MC early sign of sickle cell?	Dactylitis
Sickle cell + salmonella?	Osteomyelitis
Sickle cell dx?	Hemoglobin electrophoresis

Sickle cell peripheral smear?	Target cells, Howell-Jolly bodies (there is nothing Jolly about sickle cell)
MC inherited bleeding disorder?	Von Willenbrands disease
VWD treatment?	DDAVP (desmopressin)
MC childhood malignancy?	Leukemia
MC childhood leukemia?	ALL - Acute lymphoblastic leukemia (All kids)
ALL (Acute lymphoblastic leukemia-All kids) x-ray may show?	Mediastinal mass
Reed-Sternberg cells (owl's eye)?	Hodgkin's lymphoma
What are the B symptoms?	Fever, night sweats, and weight loss
What's cryptorchidism?	Undescended testis
Cryptorchidism complications?	Testicular cancer
Cryptorchidism treatment?	Orchiopexy as early as 6 months not before
MC congenital abnormality of the GU tract?	Cryptorchidism
MC cause of PAINLESS scrotal swelling?	Hydrocele
Hydrocele treatment?	Usually, none needed

What's Phimosis?	Inability to retract the foreskin over the glans penis
What's Paraphimosis?	Foreskin can't be pulled forward, this is emergency
Spermatic cord twist, think?	Testicular torsion
Testicular torsion physical exam?	Negative Prehn's sign and Absent cremasteric reflex
Testicular torsion best initial test is?	Testicular Doppler US
Testicular torsion treatment?	Detorsion and orchiopexy within 6 hours
MC form of primary irritant contact dermatitis?	Diaper dermatitis
MC regional lymphadenitis among children?	Cervical lymphadenitis
MC small vessel vasculitis in childhood?	Henoch-Schonlein purpura
MC bleeding disorder of childhood?	ITP
MC cause of thrombocytopenia?	ITP
Most frequently dx in a child presenting with fever is?	OM
MC cause of traveler's diarrhea?	E coli
MC cause of bronchiectasis in the US?	Cystic fibrosis

MC cause of inspiratory stridor?	Croup
MC cause of respiratory distress in a preterm infant?	Hyaline membrane disease
MC single cause of death in 1st month of life?	Hyaline membrane disease
Diphtheria tx?	Diphtheria antitoxin and abx like erythromycin and PCN
Strep pneumonia treatment?	Amoxicillin 500 bid 7-10 days
Whitish scaring of eardrum?	Tympanosclerosis
The frontal sinus is not visible on x-ray until the age?	5
A deep infection in the space between the soft palate and tonsil?	Peritonsillar abscess
Pale buggy nasal mucous?	Allergic rhinitis
By what age should a child be able to hold up her head?	3 months. roll over at 4 sit up at 6 say mama and dada at 12
A premature infant with hyaline membrane disease will have what appears on CXR?	Bilateral atelectasis or ground glass appearance.
MC cause of chronic cough in children older than three years old?	Asthma
MC birth defect?	Congenital heart defect

MC innocent murmur in early childhood?	Still's murmur
MC congenital heart defect?	Ventricular septal defect
MC cause of CHF in the first month of life?	Coarctation of aorta
MC cyanotic congenital heart defect?	Tetralogy of Fallot
MC cause of sudden cardiac death in young persons?	HOCM
How do you close a patent ductus arteriosus?	Prostaglandin inhibitor (IV indomethacin)
How do you keep a ductus areteriosis patent?	Prostaglandin E1 analogs (Alprostadil)
An atrial septal defect is usually asymptomatic until what age?	>30 years old
Continuous machinery murmur, think?	Patent ductus arteriosus
MC type of ASD?	Osmium secundum
Where is patent ductus arteriosus loudest?	Pulmonic area
What condition has blue baby syndrome?	Tetralogy of Fallot
Tetralogy of fallot x-ray will show?	Boot-shaped heart

Pulmonary

Most common (MC) preventable cause of death?	Smoking
MC tumor causing SIADH?	Small cell lung tumor
MC virus causing common cold?	Rhinovirus
Tension pneumothorax triad?	Hypotension, JVD, Absent BS
The patient presents with dyspnea you should order?	CXR, EKG, BNP (if BNP>500 95% likely CHF)
Normal PCO2 range?	35-45
Normal HCO3 levels?	22-26 mEq/L
Hypoxia levels?	96-100 normal, 91-95 mild hypoxia, 86-90 moderate to significant 85 or less severe hypoxia
MC cause of croup?	Parainfluenza virus
Barking cough, think?	Croup
Samter's triad is?	Aspirin sensitivity, nasal polyposis, and asthma
Drug of choice for pertussis?	Macrolide (Azithromycin)
MC symptoms of CAP (Community-acquired pneumonia)?	Cough with purulent sputum, fever, and dyspnea
The most common cause of fever post-op day 1-3 is?	PNA (PNA -pneumonia) (WIND) Pt is unable to take a deep breath due to the pain. The next best step is to order a CXR.
Incentive spirometry prevents what?	Atelectasis but not PNA

Treatment of choice for strep pharyngitis?	PCN VK
When can patients with strep return to the school?	After being on ABX for 24hr.
Metroplol should be used with caution in patients with which airway disease?	Reactive (Asthma)
HCAP treatment?	Cefepime+pip/tazo+Vanco
Adenosine can cause what?	Bronchospasm in pt with asthma/COPD
Wheezing could be?	Asthma, COPD, FB, Anaphylaxis, HF
Wet crackles DD (Differential diagnosis)?	HF, Pulm Edema, ARDS, hemoptysis
What's Ronchi?	Loud rumbling sounds heard on auscultation of bronchi obstructed by sputum.
Ronchi DD?	PNA/Deep FB
MC cause of cardiac arrest in children is?	Resp arrest
CPAP and Bipap are examples of?	NIPPV
In elderly patients the most common Dx's with RR >25 or SpO2 < 93% are?	Heart failure, pneumonia, COPD, PE, and asthma
MC PNA bug?	Strep Pneumo
CAP vs. HCAP run?	Drip score >4 it's HCAP

PNA site of care?	CURB65
Outpt PNA tx?	Azithromycin add Augmentin if abx /in 60days
Inpt CAP tx?	Azithromycin or doxy + ceftriaxone
Inpt HCAP tx?	Cefepime +azithro
What's Light's criterion used for?	Pleural Effusion
Peds PNA tx?	Amoxicillin
Bilateral PE is associated with?	HF
Target SpO2 for AECOPD?	88-90 if a small amount of O2 doesn't work consider PE
Medical management of AECOPD	Albuterol+Dueneb (ipatropium), 40-60mg of prednisone QD x 5,Azythro, doxy or Augmentin for OutPt, Ceftraixone, Levaquin, zosyn for inpt
4yo T40, Tachy, distress, drooling, sore throat, stridor?	Epiglottitis
Epiglottitis 3 D's	Dysphagia, Drooling, Distress
Epiglottitis bug?	HIB-Haemophilus influenza
ABX for epiglottitis?	Ceftriaxone to cover H flu, plus Vanco or Clinda

Croup age?	6m-3y
Which peds population is more likely to get epiglottitis?	Epiglottitis is more likely in un- or under-immunized children and those with drooling but no cough.
MC croup bug?	Parainfluenza virus
Croup treatment	Single-dose of oral dexamethasone, nebulized epi
DVT signs and symptoms?	Unilateral leg swelling, pain or tenderness, skin discoloration (redness), Palpation of cord-like obstruction over the vein
Homan's sign	Pain in calf upon dorsiflexion of the foot and may indicate thrombophlebitis
If PE(pulmonary embolism) pt has contrast allergy they can't get CTA, what's the next best test?	V/Q scan
PE cxr can show?	Watermarks sign and Hampton hump
PE EKG findings?	Prominent S waves in lead I, Q wave in lead III, Inverted T wave in III. "S1/Q3/T3"
PE risk stratification?	Start with PERC and WELLS
PE site of care?	PESI score
On the physical exam, pt is hemodynamically unstable with SBP<90 tx?	Thrombolysis

PE stable pt give?	Anticoags
Pregnant PE pt tx?	LMWH (Low molecular weight heparin)
Morbid obesity PE pt tx?	LMWH
Renal failure crcl<30 PE pt?	UFH (Unfractionated heparin)
Asthma exacerbation Work-up?	Pulse ox and peak flow
Asthma exacerbation tx?	ABC/IV/O2/Monitor + nebulized albuterol + PO or IV steroids. Magnesium or terbutaline if refractory. Intubate if needed.
Asthma exacerbation presents with?	Wheezing, cough, Tachy, unable to speak, pulsus paradoxus, flat diaphragm
Typically low PaCO2<35 or rapidly rising>45 indicated what in asthma pt?	Impending exhaustion
MC cause of infant hospitalization is?	RSV
RSV presentation?	A wet cough, **intercostal retractions**, scattered crackles, expiratory wheezes bilat. decreased PO intake, fever.
When do we start vaccinating pt for pneumococcal pneumonia at what age?	At 65
Watermarks sign-on CXR, think?	Pulmonary embolism

Pneumocystis Jiroveci pneumonia is treated with?	Bactrim
Thoracentesis is used to diagnose what?	Pulmonary embolism
Long cough after URI?	Acute bronchitis
Acute bronchitis treatment?	Supportive
What's Asthma?	Reversible hyperirritability of the tracheobronchial tree
Asthma presenting triad?	Wheezing, Cough, SOB
Treatment for asthma pt with PEFR<50%?	Admit them
What's Samter's triad?	Asthma, Nasal polyps and ASA/NSAID allergy
Pt is status asthmaticus will present with?	Altered mental status and inability to speak in full sentences, pulsus paradoxus
The gold standard for dx Asthma?	PFTs
What pulse ox is indicative of respiratory distress?	<90%
1st line treatment for acute asthma?	SABA - Albuterol
Anticholinergics used in asthma?	Ipratropium, side effects are thirst, dry, urinary retention, dysphagia
Pt with cystic fibrosis and Pneumonia, what bug is involved?	Pseudomonas

Cromolyn is used for?	Prophylaxis in asthma and exercise, cold air
Side effects of Beclomethasone?	Thrush
Montelukast is used for?	Asthma caused by allergic rhinitis/aspirin induced
Severe asthma we can add which medication?	Omalizumab
COPD pt <40 could have what deficiency?	A-1 antitrypsin
Emphysema is?	A condition in which the air sacs of the lungs are damaged and enlarged, causing breathlessness. INCREASED AIR TRAPPING
Croup x-ray sign?	Steeple sign
When should the nebulized epinephrine be used in the treatment of croup?	Severe cases
MC risk factor for COPD?	Smoking
COPD is what kind of airflow obstruction?	Largely irreversible
Emphysema MC sign?	Dyspnea - accessory muscle use, prolonged expiration, decreased fremitus
Emphysema ABG?	Respiratory alkalosis
Chronic bronchitis abg?	Respiratory acidosis
Barrel chest and pursed-lip breathing are seen with?	Emphysema

Pink puffers, think?	Emphysema
Blue bloaters refer to?	Chronic bronchitis
Emphysema will have what vascular markings on CT scan?	Decreased, flat diaphragm, BULLAE
Asthma Mild vs Mild persistent?	What are the nocturnal symptoms? If 2 or less a month it's mild if 3-4 it's mild persistent.
How to differentiate asthma classifications by FEV1?	Mild asthmas have FEV1>80, moderate 60-80, and severe<60.
Pt presents with a cough that lasts longer than 5 days?	Bronchitis
What's the only medical therapy proven to decrease the mortality in COPD pt?	Oxygen
In pt with OSA what wakes them up from sleep?	Hypoxia
OSA dx?	Polysomnography
OSA tx?	Mild to moderate CPAP, if severe BiPAP
What's Narcolepsy?	Excessive sleepiness during the day, sleep attacks, a major cause of MVAs
Narcolepsy tx?	Modafinil planned naps during the day.
MC cause of neonatal pneumonia?	Group B strep
MC cause of CAP?	S. Pneumo

MC cause of atypical walking pneumonia?	Mycoplasma
Mycoplasma pneumonia is usually seen in which group of people?	College and military
Legionella is associated with?	Cooling towers, AC, contaminated water supplies
MC bug in alcoholics with PNA?	Klebsiella
Aspiration PNA bugs?	Anaerobes
Rusty sputum sample?	S. Pneumo
Currant jelly sputum sample?	Klebsiella
Foul-smelling sputum sample?	Anaerobes
What meds can exacerbate COPD?	BB, decongestant, sedatives
COPD treatment?	Smoking cessation, pneumococcal and flu vaccines, systemic or inhaled corticosteroids, oxygen, inhaled beta-agonists and anticholinergics
What's the hallmark of chronic bronchitis?	Productive cough
Best meds for COPD tx?	Combo anticholanrgic/B2 ipatropium/albuterol
Anticholinergics CI (contraindications)?	BPH, glaucoma
Albuterol CI?	Severe CAD, DM, hyperglycemia, hyper T-graves

Abx for COPD exacerbation?	Azithromycin
Transmural inflammation, think?	Bronchiectasis - medium size bronchi
MC bug in bronchiectasis if not due to the CF?	H flu. recurrent/chronic lung infection
MCC of Bronchiectasis in the USA?	Cystic fibrosis due to pseudomonas
TB clinical symptoms?	Fever, night sweats, weight loss, malaise, cough
TB x-ray findings?	Ghon complex
TB dx?	CXR, Acid-fast bacilli, PCR, PPD skin test
Green sputum sample, think?	HiB or Pseudomonas
If pt is being treated for TB, which medication can turn his body fluids (urine, sweat) orange?	Rifampin
MC chronic disease in childhood?	Asthma
Will asthma have hyper or hyporesonance?	Hyper resonance
Best way to assess the severity of asthma and patient response in the ER?	Peak Expiratory Flow Rate (PEFR)
What PEFR % indicates a good response to the treatment?	>15%
Red-green vision loss and optic neuritis are side effects of which medication used for TB treatment?	Ethambutol

ABG is asthma exacerbation?	Respiratory alkalosis
Examples of systemic corticosteroids?	Prednisone, Methylprednisone, Prednisolone
Examples of inhaled corticosteroids?	Beclomethasone, Flunisolide, Triamcinolone
Treatment for intermittent asthma?	Step 1 (SABA - Albuterol)
Treatment for mild persistent asthma?	Step 2 low dose ICS (Fluticasone)
Hyaline membrane disease aka?	RDS respiratory distress syndrome
What causes RDS?	Pulmonary surfactant deficiency
Pulm HTN EKG findings?	Rt axis peaked p wave, RV strain V1 super tall peak
Hypoventilation syndrome?	Pickwickian syndrome - daytime hyperCARBIA and hypoxemia.
Hypoventilation syndrome diagnosis?	BMI>30, PaCO2 >45, PaO2<70
Which resistance is seen with Hypoventilation syndrome?	Leptin great predictor of hypercapnia
Hypoventilation syndrome treatment?	CPAP, weight loss
"Honeycombing lung" on x-ray or CT?	Interstitial pulmonary fibrosis. GROUND GLASS opacities
Physical exam in pulm fibrosis?	Fine BIBASILAR crackles, clubbing in fingers, cyanosis
MC respiratory disease of premature infants?	RDS
Sx of RDS?	Decreased breath sounds with crackles

RDS cxr will show?	Diffuse bilateral atelectasis (ground glass appearance) and **diaphragm doming**
Cystic fibrosis (CF) has what type of inheritance?	Autosomal recessive
You should suspect cystic fibrosis if the full-term infant presents with what?	Meconium ileus
Pt with CF will have what kind of stool?	Bulky pale/foul-smelling stool
MC infecting bug in pt with CF?	Pseudomonas
How is CF diagnosed, which test?	Sweat chloride test >60mmoi/L
MC cause of Bronchiectasis in the USA?	Cystic fibrosis
5 examples of obstructive lung disorders?	Asthma, COPD, Bronchiectasis, CF and Coal workers pneumoconiosis
Pulm fibrosis treatment?	Lung transplant
Inhalation of mineral dust causes what disease?	Pneumoconiosis
Silicosis is seen with inhalation?	Silica dust (mining, granite work)
Silicosis dx on cxr?	Multiple small nodular opacities in upper lobes
What kind of calcifications are seen with silicosis?	Eggshell calcifications of the hilar and mediastinal nodes **(Silicon eggs)**
What's Caplan syndrome?	Rheumatoid arthritis and coal workers pneumoconiosis

A person that works with fluorescent light bulbs can develop?	Berylliosis
Berylliosis can increase the risk for which cancers?	Lung, stomach, and colon
What other jobs are associated with the development of Berylliosis?	Electronic, aerospace, ceramics, and dye industry.
Cotton exposure can lead to what lung disease?	Byssinosis
Asbestosis affects which lung lobes?	Lower lobes (TB is upper)
Asbestosis can cause what?	MC bronchogenic carcinoma, mesothelioma is #2
Asbestosis CXR will show?	Pleural plaques and shaggy heart sign
Asbestosis biopsy will show what?	**Brown rods** due to iron/protein damage
S. Pneumoniae gram stain?	Gram + cocci in pairs
Hyponatremia is seen with which type of pneumonia?	Legionella
Currant jelly sputum cavitary lesions, think which bug?	Klebsiella
Pseudomonas gram stain?	Gram neg rods
MCC of viral PNA in transplant and HIV patients?	CMV
HCAP bugs?	Pseudomonas >48 h in the hospital or within 90 days of 2 days hospital stay

Which pathogen lacks the cell wall?	Mycoplasma
MC cause of viral PNA in infants	RSV
MC cause of viral PNA in adults?	Influenza
Pseudomonas sputum?	Rusty blood-tinged
Foul-smelling sputum?	Anaerobes
In patients with lung, issues should avoid which cardiac med?	BB
With Bird/bat dropping exposure think?	Histoplasmosis
Anti-pseudomonal b-lactams?	Pip/tazo, cefepime, imipenem, ceftazadime
Sarcoidosis labs?	Elevated ACE
Bilateral hilar lymphadenopathy think?	Sarcoidosis
Sarcoidosis Tx?	Prednisone is the clear drug of choice. Few patients fail to respond.
Solitary Pulmonary Nodule?	Coin lesion; peripheral lung nodule < 3 cm
Solitary Pulmonary Nodule is most often due to?	Granulomas
MC mediastinal tumor?	Thymoma

Influenza is characterized by which symptoms?	**ABRUPT onset of fever,** HA, chills, malaise
Oral medication for the treatment of flu with/in the first 48h of unset?	Oseltamivir
Severe coughing fits are seen with which phase of pertussis?	Paroxysmal phase
In cases of significant atelectasis, the trachea may be deviated toward or away from the affected side?	Toward the affected side
MCC of lung cancer?	Smoking - adenocarcinoma
2nd MCC of lung cancer?	Asbestosis
Most lung cancers are?	NSCC 85%
Adenocarcinoma location in the lungs?	Peripheral, SCC is central
Most aggressive lung cancer?	Large cell anaplastic
Surgery is not a choice for which type of lung cancer?	Small cell lung cancer, it's aggressive typically Mets at presentation, central
Small cell lung cancer is associated with?	SVC superior vena cava syndrome (JVD, facial plethora, PROMINENT CHEST VEINS)
Small cell tx?	Chemo and radiation
Role of D-dimer in the dx of PE?	Can r/o but not r/in

PE CXR signs?	Westermark's sign: avascular markings distal to the area of embolus, Hampton's hump: wedge-shaped infiltrate
The most important initial diagnostic study for all patients with hemoptysis is a?	CXR
COPD is the MCC of which PTX?	Spontaneous (tall, thin men 20-40y/o, smokers, Marfans)
Imaging for pneumothorax?	Expiratory CXR
MC bug in post-op PNA?	Pseudomonas
Presence of noncaseating granulomas, think?	Sarcoidosis
Sarcoidosis presentation?	African America Female, Hilar Adenopathy, SOB on exertion, and fine rales on the exam. May have Hypercalcemia and Elevated ACE level
Chronic TB Usually become PPD+ within?	2-4 weeks of infection, NOT contagious
Dx of TB?	Acid-fast smear and sputum culture x 3 days: AFB cultures GOLD STANDARD
Reactivation TB will be seen in what part of the lungs in the CXR?	Apical (upper lobe)
Tx for TB?	RIPE (rifampin, isoniazid, pyrazinamide, ethambutol)
MC single cause of death in 1st month of life?	Hyaline membrane disease

MC cause of chronic cough in children older than three years old?	Asthma
Destruction of bronchial walls from the dilation of airway sacs is a result of?	Bronchiectasis
CF presentation?	A large amount of foul-smelling sputum
Wide split S2 with palpable P2, think?	Pulm HTN
Bibasilar crackles and finger clubbing?	IPF honeycombing
Increased WBC +fever+chest pain, think?	PNA
Drop-in BP w inspiration, think?	Tension PTX
PTX (pneumothorax) and tactile fremitus?	PTX will have decreased fremitus
Pleuritic CP + dyspnea + Tachycardia, think?	PE
Smokers PNA bug?	H.flu
PNA 6m-5y treatment?	Amoxicillin (mostly answer for all kids issues)
Influence A tx?	Oseltamivir
Atypical PNA tx?	Azithro

Signs of pneumothorax include?	Hyper resonance to percussion, tracheal deviation, decreased breath sounds and decreased tactile and vocal fremitus.
The cough center is located in the?	Medulla oblongata
Nocturnal coughing may indicate?	Asthma, GERD, postnasal drip, or CHF.
Cough and dyspnea on exertion suggest a?	Cardiac etiology
Elevated cold agglutinin titer is seen with?	Mycoplasma pneumonia
Amiodarone FDA boxed warning?	Can cause irreversible Pulmonary Fibrosis
PaO2/FiO2 <300, think?	ARDS
PJP CXR will show?	Difuse or bilateral **PERIhilar** infiltrates
Active TB pt should be isolated for how long?	At least 2 weeks following the treatment
Transudative fluid in PE will show?	Low protein and normal LDH
Exudative fluid in PE will show?	High protein and LDH
Which type of lung cancer is typically centrally located?	Squamous cell carcinoma
Pectus carinatum, think?	Pigeon chest

Bronchiectasis is also MCC of?	Massive hemoptysis
Bronchiectasis Abx?	Empiric Amoxicillin, Pseudomonas coverage
Bronchiectasis CT will show?	Tram-track appearance
MCC of secondary pulm HTN?	COPD
DX gold standard for pulm HTN?	Rt side cath
Pulm HTN treatment?	Milrinone, sildenafil if non-reactive, CCB is 1st line if vasoactive
A most common location for pleural effusion?	Costophranic angles
The flattened diagram on CXR, think?	COPD
Blebs on CXR. Think?	COPD
Curly B-lines on CXR, think?	CHF (Congestive heart failure)
Cephalizations of vessels on CXR, think?	CHF (Congestive heart failure)
Deep sulcus sign on CXR, think?	Pneumothorax
Pneumonia will show what on CXR?	Consolidations
Aortic dissection on CXR will show?	Widened mediastinum

Ophthalmology

MC (most common) type of glaucoma?	Open-angle
Strabismus should resolve by what age?	4 months if not get an optho referral
Itchy eyes are most likely?	allergic conjunctivitis
Why should we treat peds conjunctivitis?	50% is bacterial so treat even if suspected viral
Treatment for peds conjunctivitis?	Ocuflox drops 1 drop QID till clear for 2 days
Orbital cellulitis treatment?	IV ABX (Vanco, Clinda)
MC population affected by Orbital cellulitis?	Children
How to tell pre-septal cellulitis vs orbital cellulitis?	Pain with ocular movement and decreased vision will be present with orbital cellulitis
How to diagnose orbital cellulitis?	High res CT
MC bugs causing bacterial conjunctivitis?	Staph/strep
Will bacterial conjunctivitis cause vision issues?	Usually no vision changes
Bacterial conjunctivitis will present with what?	Purulent discharge glued shut on awakening, absence of ciliary injection

What bug should we think about covering in contact wearers?	Pseudomonas
Eye poring out pus, think?	Gonorrhea
What is strabismus?	Misalignment of the eyes.
Screening test for strabismus?	**Hirschberg** corneal light reflex test
Cover-uncover test is used for what?	To determine the angle of strabismus
Conservative therapy for strabismus?	Patch therapy by covering the good eye
If strabismus is not corrected by age 2 what can develop?	Amblyopia
Painful red eye with a fixed pupil describes?	Acute angle glaucoma
Associated with a **loss of central vision** and blurring of vision?	Macular degeneration
Presbyopia is what?	Age-associated loss of the ability of the eye to accommodate.
Glaucoma, left untreated, leads to?	A loss of peripheral vision (not central) and eventual blindness.
Glaucoma is the most common cause of blindness?	African Americans
Itching of the eye is not typical of acute angle glaucoma. It is more consistent with?	Allergic conjunctivitis
Painless monocular vision loss?	Central retinal artery occlusion (CRAO). The keyword is painless!

Vit A deficiencies eye exam?	Bitot spots on conjunctive
Exophthalmos is seen with?	Graves disease. It's an abnormal protrusion of the eyeball
Describe Retinitis?	Inflammation of the retina by CMV.
Associated with a loss of central vision and blurring of vision?	Macular degeneration
The gradual loss of peripheral vision?	Open-angle glaucoma
Open-angle glaucoma?	**The enlarged cup-to-disk ratio** in one or both eyes and may reveal diminished visual fields. Intraocular eye pressure (IOP) may be normal or increased.
Acute unilateral painful vision loss, vomiting, and seeing halos around lights?	Acute Angle-Closure Glaucoma
Slit-lamp examination reveals "cell and flare" in the anterior chamber, think?	Iritis
Fundoscopy will show "boxcar" look or "**cherry-red spot**"?	CRAO
What's Blepharitis?	Inflammation of both eyelids. Common in pt's with down syndrome and eczema
What's posterior Blepharitis?	Meibomian gland dysfunction
Blepharitis presentation?	Eye irritation/itching, Eyelids with burning, erythema, crusting, scaling, red-rimming of the eyelid and eyelash flaking

Anterior Blepharitis tx?	Eyelid hygiene, warm compresses, eyelid scrubbing/washing with baby shampoo.
Posterior Blepharitis tx?	Eyelid hygiene, regular massage/expression of Meibomian gland
Foreign body sensation, **tearing, red**, painful eye is consistent with?	Corneal abrasion
Corneal abrasion Fluorescein staining will show?	"ice rink" or linear abrasion. Make sure to evert the eyelid
Corneal abrasion tx?	Check visual acuity first, FB removal, a patch with large abrasions > 5 mm, but do not wear longer than 24 hours. Do not patch the eye in contact wearers→ treat with Cipro eye drops to cover pseudomonas. Give topical erythromycin, polymixin/trimethoprim, Cipro
MCC of corneal ulcers?	Bacterial - Pseudomonas
HSV keratitis will show what on the fluorescein staining?	**Branching**
HSV keratitis tx?	Topical antivirals ganciclovir, PO acyclovir
What's the infection of the lacrimal sac called?	Dacryocystitis
MC bug that causes Dacryocystitis?	S. Aureus

Dacryocystitis presentation?	Tenderness, erythema, redness to medial canthal (nasal side) of the lower lid. Maybe purulent.
What's Ectropion?	Eyelid and lashes turned outward
Ectropion happens due to relaxation of which muscle?	Orbicularis oculi muscle
Mid-dilated non-reactive pupil, think?	Glaucoma
Glaucoma vision?	Peripheral vision goes first, looks like tunnel vision
Glaucoma dx?	Increased intraocular pressure by tonometry (>21mmHg)
Glaucoma tx?	Ophthalmic emergency- refer immediately, IV acetazolamide- 1st line
What's definitive tx for glaucoma?	Laser or surgical iridectomy
MCC of Hordeolum?	S. Aureus
What's Hordeolum?	Abscess of the eyelid margin, painful warm, swollen red lump on the eyelid (PAINFUL - remember H for hurts)
Hordeolum tx?	Warm compresses are the mainstay of treatment, I+D if no spontaneous drainage after 48 hours
What is blood inside the anterior chamber of the eye called?	Hyphema

MCC of permanent legal blindness and visual loss in the elderly?	Macular degeneration
Macular degeneration presentation?	Bilateral blurred or loss of central vision (Glaucoma is the loss of peripheral vision)
Pt with Macular degeneration can see straight lines appear as bent lines, what is that called?	Metamorphopsia
Drusen spots, think?	Dry Macular degeneration
Diagnosis of wet Macular degeneration?	Fluorescein angiography
Swollen optic disc with blurred margins, think?	Papilledema
Papilledema tx?	Diuretics (acetazolamide) decreases the production of aqueous humor and CSF
What's Pterygium?	Fleshy triangular-shaped fibrovascular mass MC in the inner corner of the eye (Triangular shape inner eye think Pterygium) pinguecula is yellow(Yellow penguin)
MC type of Retinal detachment?	Rhegmatogenous
Retinal detachment presentation?	**Curtain coming down**, Photopsia (flashing lights), floaters, progressive unilateral vision loss. NOT PAINFUL
Blood and Thunder on Fundoscopy, think?	**CRVO**

MCC of new, permanent vision loss/blindness in 25-74 yr olds?	Retinopathy
Cotton wool patches and blot and dot hemorrhages, think?	Nonproliferative Retinopathy
Nonproliferative Retinopathy tx?	Strict glucose control
Proliferative Retinopathy tx?	VEGF inhibitors
Teardrop pupil, think?	Ruptured globe with iris prolapse (Ophthalmic Emergency!)
How do we check IOP?	Schiotz tonometer
Penetrating trauma to the eye treatment?	The object shouldn't be removed, don't apply pressure, shield the eye, avoid eye drops, transfer to ER for optho consult, give prophylactic abx
Eye Foreign Bodies Dx and Tx?	Evert the eyelid, stain with fluorescent, and observe with blue light (WOODS LAMP), remove if you can. Patching for 24 hours if large abrasion. Refer to optho
Rust ring removal is done with?	Rotating BURR, refer to optho
Chemical eye burn treatment?	Irrigate with saline for 30 min, shield the eye, optho referral in ER
Retinal detachment treatment?	Emergency consult with an ophthalmologist for possible laser or cryosurgery. Keep the patient supine with the head

	turned to the side of the retinal detachment.
In retinal detachment, IOP will be?	Normal or decreased
Drugs that cause macular degeneration?	Chloroquine or phenothiazine
Sudden painless loss of vision in **one eye?**	Central retinal artery occlusion
Separation of arterial flow is aka?	Box-caring (CRAO)
Perifoveal atrophy aka?	Cherry red spots
Neovascularization can be treated with?	VEGF
What's the cataract?	**Clouding of the lens** of the eye with increased in insoluble protein
Most common cataracts?	Senile
Cataract treatment?	Lens replacement with capsular extraction
Glaucoma is defined as?	Increased IOP with optic nerve damage
MC type of glaucoma?	Open-angle. Pt will usually be AA >40 years old. PERIPHERAL VISION LOSS
Closed-angle glaucoma presentation?	Painful eye and vision loss, **steamy cornea, and fixed mix-dilated pupil.** Up IOP, N/V/diaphoresis. (Pain is worst in a dark room) This is an optho emergency.
Closed-angle glaucoma treatment?	IV carbonic anhydrase inhibitor (**acetazolamide**) topical BB, and osmotic diuresis (mannitol)

Dacrostenosis vs. dacryocystitis?	Cystitis is infection, pain-swelling tenderness. Warm compressors and abx
Inflammation of the Meibomian glands and a common cause of recurrent conjunctivitis?	Posterior Blepharitis
Entropion affects which muscle?	Orbicularis oculi
Copious watery eye discharge, think?	Viral conjunctivitis adenovirus likely highly contagious swimming pools, ipsilateral tender preauricular lymphadenopathy
Viral conjunctivitis treatment?	Normal saline bid for 2 weeks eye lavage.
Sulfonamide drops are used for?	To prevent viral conjunctivitis from going bacterial
Orbital cellulitis presentation?	Abrupt onset of fever, proptosis, restriction of extraocular movements, and swelling with redness of the lids.
Neisseria vs chlamydia in bacterial conjunctivitis?	N.G. is unilateral copious PURULANT discharge where chlamydia is MUCOPURULENT
Bacterial conjunctivitis tx?	Topical sulfonamide (trimethoprim with polymixin B) or Gentamicin or Erythromycin ointment. Drops>ointments
Causes of papilledema?	Elevated intraocular pressure (e.g., glaucoma) leads to an enlarged cup. Malignant HTN, strokes, subdural hematoma and pseudotumor cerebri

Causes of transient vision loss?	TIA, amaurosis fugax and Giant cell arteritis
Sudden vision loss causes?	CRVO, optic neuropathy (MS), papillitis and retrobulbar neuritis
What's retrobulbar neuritis?	An inflammatory process of the optic nerve behind the eyeball
Cupping of the optic disc, think?	Open-angle glaucoma
Papilledema Treatment?	Acetazolamide
Dendritic lesions are seen with?	Herpes Keratitis
Retinal hemorrhages and hyphema in a baby, think?	Shaken baby syndrome
Presbyopia is an?	Age-associated loss of the ability of the eye to accommodate.
What's the infection of the lacrimal sac called?	Dacryocystitis
Patient reports seeing flashing lights and floaters, think?	Retinal detachment
What's the medical term used to describe the difference between the sizes of the pupils of the eyes?	Anisocoria. Defined by a difference of 0.4 mm or more between the sizes of the pupils of the eyes.
What's the medical term used to describe drooping or falling of the upper eyelid?	Ptosis
Miosis describes what?	Pinpoint pupil

Ptosis + Miosis + anhydrases, think?	Horner's syndrome
Curtain coming down and **then going back up,** think?	Amaurosis fugax
What cup to disc ratio is indicative of glaucoma?	>0.5
Amsler grid is used to test what?	Metamorphopsia
What is Chalazion?	Painless nodule on the eyelid
Ishihara plates are used to test what?	Color blindness
Macular degeneration will have what kind of deposits on the fundal exam?	Drusen deposits

Good luck on your test! You have studied hard and I'm sure you will do just fine, remember "Thousand's and thousand's of students done this before you, so can you PERIOD". **PLEASE DO ME A HUGE FAVOR AND LEAVE AN AMAZON COMMENT FOR THE BOOK. THAT HELPS ME A LOT AND LET'S OTHER STUDENTS KNOW IF YOU FOUND THIS BOOK HELPFUL. THANK YOU!!!!!!**

GU

Which diuretic holds on to calcium?	HCTZ. Loops dispose of the Ca
MC tumor causing SIADH?	Small cell lung tumor
MCC of Balanitis?	Candida Albicans
Balanitis tx for a fungal cause?	Clotrimazole 1%
What's BPH?	Prostate hyperplasia (enlargement of the transitional zone) leads to bladder outlet obstruction
MC cause of UTI?	E.Coli
What is the definitive treatment for BPH?	TURP
MC STI in the USA?	Chlamydia
For kidney stones order which imaging test?	CT without contrast
Inflammation of the glans penis is called?	Balanitis
Erectile dysfunction can occur with which heart medication?	Beta-blockers
Kidney stones are mostly made up of what?	Calcium (Gallbladder stones from cholesterol)
Tea colored urine, think?	Hepatitis
In asymptomatic individuals the best initial test for the evaluation of hematuria?	Urine culture
Which tumor markers are elevated in testicular cancer?	Serum alpha-fetoprotein

MC presenting area of prostate cancer?	Peripheral zone
What's Wilms tumor?	Unilateral renal mass is seen in children
BUN/Cre ration is >20:1, think?	Pre-renal
GFR is 38, this is what stage of Chronic kidney disease?	**Stage 3 (GFR 30-59)**. Stage 1. GFR >90, stage 2. GFR 60-89, stage 4. GFR 15-29, stage 5 GFR <15
UA shows **muddy** brown cast, think?	**ATN** Acute Tubular necrosis (MUDDY **ATM** no money)
Diabetes insipidus (DI) think low or high Na?	High Na (Hypernatremia)
With ABG think?	**ROME** (respiratory opposite pH and rest, Metabolic even all going in the same direction up or down)
Metabolic acidosis ABG will show?	All 3 down (pH <7.35, pCO2 <35, HCO3 < 22)
Metabolic Alkalosis ABG will show?	All 3 up (pH >7.45, pCO2 >45, HCO3 >26)
Respiratory Alkalosis ABG will show?	**Think ROME** (pH is the first part you look at when applying ROME, in **alkalosis pH will be high** so therefore HCO3 will be low) pH >7.45, PCO2 <35, HCO3 <22
Risk factors for erectile dysfunction (ED)?	Hypertension, Depression, Psychological, CAD, DM
The penis is curved in the middle, this is what?	Peyronie's disease (cased by fibrous tissue)

What's a cystocele?	Bladder prolapse (posterior bladder herniation into the anterior vagina)
Pelvic organ prolapse PE?	Bulging mass that increases with Valsalva
Pelvic organ prolapse tx?	Kegels, pessaries, surgery (surgery only if symptomatic)
Cystocele PE?	Visualization of downward movement of the anterior vaginal wall with Valsalva.
What is uterine prolapse?	Uterine herniation into the vagina
Which incontinence will have high PVR?	Overflow
Flank pain radiating to the groin, think?	Kidney stones
What is phrens sign?	Pain relieved by elevating the scrotum
Positive Prehn's sign, think?	Epididymitis
CVA tenderness, think?	Pyelonephritis
Pyelonephritis tx?	Outpatient if stable give Bactrim or Ciprofloxacin
What is stress incontinence?	Urine leakage due to increased intra-abdominal pressure
Urine leakage from sneezing or laughing?	Stress incontinence
Stress incontinence tx?	Kegels/Pelvic floor exercises
Overactive bladder aka?	Urge incontinence

Urge incontinence is due to?	Detrusor muscle overactivity
Urge incontinence tx?	Bladder training, Detrol or **Oxybutynin**
The underactive bladder will cause what kind of incontinence?	Overflow incontinence
Overflow incontinence other causes?	BPH, strictures
Overflow incontinence presentation?	Increased post-void residual >200mL, dribbling
MCC of UTIs in the hospital?	Indwelling catheters or GU instrumentation
Aldosterone works where?	Distal convoluted tubes
What's cryptorchidism?	Undescended testis
Cryptorchidism complications?	Testicular cancer
Cryptorchidism treatment?	Orchiopexy as early as 6 months not before
MC congenital abnormality of the GU tract?	Cryptorchidism
MC cause of PAINLESS scrotal swelling?	Hydrocele
Hydrocele treatment?	Usually, none needed
What's Phimosis?	Inability to retract the foreskin over the glans penis
What's **Parap**himosis?	Foreskin can't be pulled forward, this is **emergency**
Spermatic **cord twist**, think?	Testicular **torsion**

Testicular torsion physical exam?	Negative Prehn's sign and Absent cremasteric reflex
Testicular torsion best initial test is?	Testicular Doppler US
Testicular torsion treatment?	Detorsion and orchiopexy within 6 hours
The classic sign of urinary retention in an elderly patient?	Confusion
MC solid tumor in young men 15-40?	Testicular Carcinoma
MC type of testicular carcinoma is?	Seminomatous **germ cell** tumors
Nonseminomas associated with increased?	Serum alpha-fetoprotein increased B-hCG
Seminomas may spread to the?	Bone
Dx of testicular cancer?	The scrotal US
MC Bladder Carcinoma type?	**Transitional** cell carcinoma (transition to the bladder)
Dx of bladder cancer?	Cystoscopy - looking into the urinary bladder with a bx.
Staging bladder cancer and initial treatment?	Transurethral resection is used to stage the tumor as well as being the initial treatment
Complaining of **painless hematuria in the elderly smoker**?	Bladder cancer
What's special about bladder cancer?	Most respond well to treatment, however, it has the highest rate of recurrences of all cancers
RCC (renal cell carcinoma) sx triad?	Hematuria, flank/abdominal pain, palpable mass

RCC, Imaging of choice?	CT
Name two medications that can treat BPH?	Tamsulosin (**Flo**max), Finaste**ride**
MCC of CKD (chronic kidney disease)?	DM
UA for CKD will show?	Broad waxy casts
Small kidney on the US?	CKD classic, if large it's due to DM
Which electrolyte should be controlled during CKD?	Control phosphate
Staghorn calculi, think?	Struvite stones
Waxy casts, think?	Chronic end-stage renal disease
CKD causes?	DM, HTN, glomerulonephritis
Rubbery firm prostate is?	BPH starts with the 5-A finasteride or A-1 blocker Flomax.
Gradual onset unilateral scrotal pain?	Epididymitis, increased Doppler flow, relief with phrens sign.
HTN + **hematuria +periorbital edema**?	Poststreptococcal glomerulonephritis AKI
MCC of **painless scrotal swelling**?	Hydrocele gets worst with Valsalva
Viagra shouldn't be taken with what other medication?	Nitroglycerin
Polycystic kidney triad?	HTN, hematuria, flank pain dx with the US

Polycystic kidney tx?	ACEi correct the BP
Polycystic kidney is associated with?	Berry aneurysm in the brain and intracerebral hemorrhage
MC prostate cancer?	Adenocarcinoma
Renal stones in kids?	Cystine
What causes flank pain?	Renal pelvic or superior urethral obstruction
Left-sided varicocele can be seen with?	RCC
MCC of secondary HTN?	RAAS activation
ACE CI (contraindications)?	Bilateral stenosis or solitary kidney
Varicocele on the right side in kids<10, think?	Retroperitoneal malignancy
Acute onset hematuria and facial edema in a child?	Post GAS glomerulonephritis
MCC of nephrOTIC syndrome in children?	Minimal change disease
MC type of acute renal failure?	Pre-renal
Prostate cancer site?	Peripheral zone
BPH MC site?	Transitional zone
The first sign of DM kidney damage is what?	Microalbuminuria
Normal microalbumin level?	<30 is normal, 30-300 early KD, >300 is kidney damage

In asymptomatic individuals, the initial test for the evaluation of hematuria is a?	Urine culture
Overflow incontinence usually presents with?	Constant leakage of urine with a postvoid residual greater than 200 ml.
A definitive diagnosis of testicular cancer?	Radical inguinal orchiectomy
A recent URI may cause hematuria in a patient with?	IgA nephropathy (Berger disease).
Hemoptysis combined with hematuria is a symptom of?	Goodpasture syndrome
A tender, boggy prostate is a sign of?	Prostatitis
Hypertension and peripheral edema are common findings with?	Glomerulonephritis
Pyuria is what?	Presence of white cells in the urine, usually indicating infection, >4 or 5 WBC
If you hold a flashlight against hydrocele will it transilluminate?	Yes
Oval fat bodies, if present, are due to lipiduria, as seen in?	Nephr**otic** syndrome (OTIC-OVAL)
Is varicocele MC on the left or right side?	On the left
Bag of worms, think?	**Varicocele**
Blue dot sign is seen with?	Testicular Torsion (This is a surgical emergency)

HCTZ (hydrochlorothiazide) works on?	Distal dilated tubules
HCTZ side effects?	(HyperGLUC) hyperGlycemia, hyperLipidemia, hyperUricemia, hyperCalcemia.
Elevated postvoid residual volume, think?	Overflow incontinence
What test should be obtained before placing a Foley catheter if the urethral injury is suspected?	Retrograde UrethroGram
Urethral trauma classic sign?	Blood at the meatus
Cremasteric reflex will be absent with?	Testicular Torsion (This is a surgical emergency)
MC cause of prerenal failure?	Dehydration
MC long term complications of polycystic kidney disease?	Hypertension and renal failure
This type of incontinence results from an overactive detrusor muscle?	Urge
What hematological disorder may cause priapism?	Sickle cell crisis
MC form of nephrotic syndrome?	Membranous glomerulonephritis
MC type of renal cell carcinoma?	Clear cell
In testicular torsion, surgery must be done within what time frame?	4-6 hours

What type of nephropathy is associated with Hodgkin's lymphoma?	Minimal change nephropathy
Pt presents with hypertension and azotemia. What is his most likely diagnosis?	Polycystic kidney disease
Bilateral hydronephrosis leads to what type of renal failure?	Post renal failure due to obstruction
If neither testes are palpable at birth, obtain?	Ultrasound and karyotype promptly
Postcoital UTI tx?	Single-dose TMP-SMX or cephalexin may reduce the frequency of UTI in sexually active women
MC cause of recurrent cystitis in men?	Chronic bacterial prostatitis
Testicular torsion is MC seen in which pt age group?	Under 20
Normal pH of Blood is?	7.35-7.45
Lossing HCO3 will cause?	Metabolic acidosis
Increased bicarb can lead to?	Met alkalosis
Varicocele on the right side in kids<10, think?	Retroperitoneal malignancy
When do we start screening for prostate cancer?	At age 50 with the PSA level.
What PSA level should indicate further workup for prostate cancer?	> 4.0

Endocrine

Most common pituitary microadenoma?	Prolactinoma most are nonfunctional
Where is the thymus gland found?	Behind the sternum, active only until puberty after it turns into fat. Produces Thymosin-> T-cell development
What are hormones?	They are chemical messengers created by endocrine glands
What are glands?	Group of cells that produce/secrete chemicals into the body
What are the 5 hypothalamic releasing hormones?	TRH, CRH, GnRH, GHRH, PRH
What connects the pituitary with the hypothalamus?	Infundibulum
Which two hormones are produced in the posterior pituitary gland?	ADH aka Vasopressin and Oxytocin
Disease in the posterior pituitary will cause?	Disorder of water homeostasis
Which hormone inhibits the release of calcium from the bones?	Calcitonin
Hypo ADH, think?	Diabetes insipidus
Hyper ADH, think?	SIADH
Increase in FSH leads to?	Menopause
Which hormone stimulates the release of calcium from the bones?	Parathyroid PTH

Hyper PTH leads to?	Hypercalcemia (PTH=Ca, if one goes up the other one, will as well)
Pancreatic islet cells are responsible for the production of?	Glucagon
Fight or flight response is regulated by which hormone?	Cortisol from Adrenal gland
Macroadenomas are what size?	>1cm
Bitemporal Hemianopia is seen with?	The mass effect of pituitary tumor
Bitemporal Hemianopia is caused by impingement of what?	Optic chiasm
What is the best imaging for pit tumors?	MRI
PRL secretion is pulsatile and peaks during?	REM sleep
Increase in PRL during nursing causes what?	Milk production and release of oxytocin, Decrease in GnRH and sex drive, decrease in LH and FSH resulting in ovulation suppression
If the lab results show PRL>200, think?	Prolactinoma
Typical triad of prolactinoma presentations in a woman?	Amenorrhea, Galactorrhea, and infertility
When testing for hypothyroidism which labs do we order?	TSH and T4

What is the normal prolactin level?	<20
Name the two drugs that are used for the treatment of hyperprolactinomas?	Cabergoline and Bromocriptine (Dopamine receptor agonist)
What is the most abundant anterior pituitary hormone?	Growth hormone
Describe the process of Glycogenolysis?	GH stimulates the liver to break down glycogen into glucose fueling growth effect.
Hypoglycemia is seen with a deficiency in which hormone?	Growth hormone (GH)
What happens when calcium level is high in the blood?	The Parathyroid gland stops making PTH and Calcitonin is released to lower the blood Calcium level.
Deficiency in calcium can lead to what when it comes to the muscle system?	Cramps and weakness
Normal serum Mg is required for optimal secretion of which hormone?	PTH
Osteoclast vs osteoblast?	The osteoclast is breaking down the bones for calcium and osteoblast are building new bone (B for the build)
Name some causes of hypercalcemia?	Menopause, Men type I, Neck radiation and Lithium use
What is the most common cause (MCC) of hyperparathyroidism?	Parathyroid adenoma 80%
What is a chvostek sign?	Contraction of ipsilateral facial muscles after percussion over the facial nerve. It is considered

	a clinical indicator of hypocalcemia
What is Trousseau's sign?	Carpopedal spasm caused by inflating the blood-pressure cuff to a level above systolic pressure for 3 minutes.
Hypocalcemia will show what on the EKG?	Prolonged QT and T wave abnormalities
MCC of (MEN) multiple endocrine neoplasias?	Gene mutation (it's Autosomal dominant)
In MEN type I what is the most common syndrome seen?	Wermer's syndrome
What are the 3 P's seen with patients with MEN type I?	Pit. Adenoma, Parathyroid hyperplasia, and Pancreatic tumors
With MEN type 2a think 2 PM?	Parathyroid hyperplasia, Pheochromocytoma, and Medullary thyroid carcinoma
Where does the pheochromocytoma originate?	Adrenal medulla and produces Cathacolamines Dacryocystitis presentation
With MEN type 2b, think 3MP?	Medullary thyroid carcinoma, Mucosal Neuromas, Marfans, Pheochromocytoma
Testosterone inhibits the production of which hormones?	LH and FSH in the anterior pit
What two syndromes are seen with primary hypogonadism?	Klinefelter's and Noonan's syndrome
What is the most common cause of primary hypogonadism?	Klinefelter's syndrome (XXY syndrome)

Webbed neck, high hairline, low set ears, short stature, and ptosis describes which syndrome?	Noonan's syndrome
Which syndrome is seen with secondary hypogonadism?	Prader-Willi syndrome
Patients with 6 fingers or toes are likely to have which syndrome?	Laurence-Moon syndrome
Patients with red-green blindness are likely to have which syndrome?	Kaplan syndrome
Patient with low Testosterone and low LH, think?	Pit tumor
All steroids are synthesized from?	Cholesterol
The patient has a fruity breath that should make you think?	Diabetes insipidus (presents with ketoacidosis)
How do we diagnose diabetes?	A single reading of BG >200 nonfasting or two fasting readings >126, A1C > 6.5
How does metformin work?	By decreasing gluconeogenesis and increasing insulin sensitivity
What are the major side effects of metformin?	Lactic acidosis and GI upset
At what creatinine level should metformin be stopped?	M >1.5 and F >1.4
Which organ is responsible for glucose regulation?	Pancreas
Which pancreas cells secrete somatostatin?	Delta cells (Alpha secrete glucagon, beta insulin)

What does glucagon do?	Maintain glucose level between meals or during fasting, initiates gluconeogenesis
Pt with hypoglycemia will have increased or decreased glucagon?	Increased
What is the classical presentation of DM type I?	Polyuria, polydipsia, weight loss and DKA
What is Diabulimia?	Eating disorder in which people with type 1 diabetes deliberately give themselves less insulin than they need or stop taking it altogether for the purpose of weight loss.
MC cause of hyperthyroidism?	Graves disease
MC cause of hypothyroidism in the USA?	Hashimoto's disease
MC cause of hypothyroidism Worldwide?	Iodine deficiency
MC thyroid cancer?	Papillary
MC cause of adrenal insufficiency?	Exogenous glucocorticoid use
MC cause of Cushing's syndrome?	Exogenous glucocorticoid use
MC complication from DM?	Neuropathy
If a patient is taking insulin, should the patient take it on the day of surgery?	No, only half of the long-acting insulin (e.g., Lente) and start D5NS IV; check glucose levels often preoperatively, operatively, and postoperatively

What is Cushing's syndrome?	Excessive cortisol production
Primary hypogonadism?	High FSH and low testosterone
No breast and no uterus?	46xy
Hyperprolactinoma labs?	Decreased LH/FSH and increased PRL get an MRI
Hyperprolactinoma tx?	Transsphenoidal surgery
What's Sheehan's syndrome?	Severe postpartum hemorrhage causing ischemic necrosis of anterior pituitary
Which medication can stimulate Gonadotrophin secretion?	Clomiphene
Which drug can cause nephrogenic DI?	Lithium
DI labs?	Hypercalcemia and hypokalemia (DI pt Love Milk and hate bananas)
Decreased PO water intake leads to?	Hypernatremia (less water more Na)
Diagnosing diabetes insipidus?	Fluid deprivation test
The next step in diagnosing diabetes insipidus after a fluid starvation test keeps producing diluted urine?	desmopressin (ADH) stimulation (central- if it responds to ADH it's working means it's central) however if it keeps with diluted its nephrogenic

Treatment for central DI?	Desmopressin
Treatment for nephrogenic DI?	HCTZ, indomethacin, amiloride, hydration
Most severe DI complications?	Cerebral Edema
Hypothyroidism labs?	Decreased T4 and increased TSH (remember TSH and Thyroid are vs if TSH is high its hypothyroidism)
Hypothyroidism treatment?	Levothyroxine
Will patients with hyperthyroidism have an intolerance to the heat or cold?	Heat
MC cause of hyperparathyroidism?	Parathyroid adenoma
MC cause of secondary hyperparathyroidism?	Chronic kidney failure
MC initial presentation of type 1 diabetes mellitus?	DKA
Type 1 DM is caused by?	Pancreatic beta-cell destruction
Hyperparathyroidism labs will show?	Increased PTH and Ca, decreased P
Which carcinoma is associated with hypercalcemia due to secretion of parathyroid hormone-related peptide (PTHrp) as well as bone destruction?	Squamous cell carcinoma

Hyperparathyroidism think?	Bones, stones, abdominal groans, psychic moans, with fatigue overtones.
Imaging test of choice for Hyperparathyroidism?	US
Hyperthyroid labs will show?	Low TSH and high T4
MC type of thyroid cancer	Papillary carcinoma (most popular thyroid cancer)
Initial tests during diagnostic workup for thyroid cancer?	Thyroid function tests and ultrasound
HLA-DR4?	Diabetes mellitus type 1, rheumatoid arthritis, Addison disease
In patients with decreased TSH perform which scan?	A radionuclide thyroid scan should be performed to determine whether or not the nodule is functioning
Where is the drainage of the left adrenal vein?	Left renal vein
Where is the drainage of the right adrenal vein?	Inferior vena cava
Adrenal tumor labs will show?	High cortisol, low ACTH, no suppression with low-dose or high-dose dexamethasone
Catecholamine-secreting adrenal tumor?	Pheochromocytoma
Pheochromocytomas are catecholamine-secreting tumors that arise from?	Chromaffin cells of the adrenal medulla
Pheochromocytoma triad presentation?	Palpitations, Headaches, Excessive sweating

Dx of pheochromocytoma?	24 hr urinary catecholamine
Dx imaging for the pheochromocytoma?	CT/MRI of abd
Tx for pheochromocytoma?	Phenoxybenzamine (alpha-blocker) for 10-14 days pro-op then propranolol.
Acromegaly tests?	Inc insulin-like growth factor (screening), confirm with oral glucose suppression test if inc GH it's positive for acromegaly
Acromegaly treatment?	Pituitary adenoma resection
Addison's disease primary?	Adrenal gland destruction lack of cortisol and aldosterone.
MMC of secondary Addison's?	Steroid use
Addison's presentation?	hypoNa, hyperK,
Addison's Testing?	8 am test high dose ACTH stimulation which should bring up cortisol if is still low next step would be CRH stimulation test to differentiate btw primary gland and secondary pit issue. If ACTH is up but cortisol is down that primary, secondary they are both down (LOW CORTISONE AT THE END IS PIT PROBLEM)
Occurs in patients with thyroid disease and is associated with localized areas of swelling?	Pretibial myxedema

Addison's tx?	Hydrocortisone (glucocorticoid) + fludrocortisone (mineralocorticoid). Only give glucocorticoids in secondary
MCC Cushing's syndrome?	Exogenous steroid administration
Cushing's vs Addison's when comes to the pit?	In Addison's pit didn't release ACTH in Cushing it has released too much
What can cause excess ACTH secretion?	Small cell lung cancer
Cushing's test?	Low dose dexamethasone suppression test - normal is the suppression of cortisol if still inc in 24-hour urine its Cushing's
Cushing's tx?	Surgical resection of the tumor
MC type of DI?	Central (no ADH production)
DI testing?	Fluid deprivation test - DI continues to make diluted urine, Desmopressin test with have a response with ADH that's central, where nephrogenic will still make dilute (CENTRAL RESPONDS TO THE DESMOPRESSIN)
BG<50 is indicative of what?	Hypoglycemia start with IV bolus of D50 or inject glucagon
The dawn phenomenon is what?	A nocturnal release of growth hormone, which may cause blood glucose level elevations before breakfast in the client

	with diabetes mellitus. Treatment includes administering an evening dose of intermediate-acting insulin at 10 pm.
Hyperparathyroidism test?	24 h urine calcium level
Hyperparathyroidism and reflexes?	vs. Meaning, if hyper-reflexes are seen on PE think decreased PTH (reflex and Calcium are also vs)
Pretibial myxedema should make you think of what diagnosis?	Graves
Graves disease treatment?	Treated by surgical removal of the thyroid or partial destruction of thyroid with radioactive iodine
TSH pit adenoma?	TSH and T4 are both increased
MC thyroid cancer after radiation exposure?	Papillary mc in young female
Most aggressive thyroid cancer?	Anaplastic
Hypocalcemia Tx?	Calcium gluconate IV, mild Po calcium and Vit D
Patients that underwent post transsphenoidal resection are at risk for?	Central DI down ADH
MCC of nephrogenic DI?	Lithium. Kidneys don't respond to the ADH

Nephrogenic DI tx?	Sodium restriction and thiazide diuretic
Goal TSH after thyroidectomy?	0.1-2
Destruction of the pancreatic beta-cells would result in?	Type 1 DM
Goal 2 h postprandial sugar level?	<180
Goal BP in DM?	<140/90
Goal LDL in DM?	<100
Metformin can cause what?	Lactic acidosis
When should Metformin be d/c?	Stop if Cr>1.5M or 1.4F
For pt that can't take metformin, give?	Glipizide
Initial Insulin Therapy?	Bedtime basal
Darkening of the skin may point toward?	Addison disease as a potential cause.
If the pt with Graves disease is taking PTU what should we monitor?	Liver failure and leukopenia
Which hormones increase the HR?	Epi and Norepi
Which hormone decreases the HR?	Acetylcholine regulated by the vagus nerve

1st line med for tx of Acromegaly?	Octreotide
Hypoparathyroidism treatment?	IV calcium gluconate, vit D
Presents classically as HTN with hypokalemia?	Aldosteronism
This med stimulates pancreatic beta-cell insulin release?	Sulfonylureas
Sulfonylureas' side effect?	Hypoglycemia
Thiazolidinediones increase insulin sensitivity in?	Peripheral receptor site adipose and muscle has no effect on pancreatic beta cells
Give a couple of examples of Thiazolidinediones?	Pioglitazone (Actos), Rosiglitazone (Avandia)
MC risk factor for thyroid carcinoma is?	Radiation exposure
What is the endocrine disease that leads to hypernatremia?	Diabetes insipidus
Hyperpigmentation due to elevated ACTH is seen with?	Addison disease
Buffalo hump and moon face, think?	Hypercortisolism
Prolonged use of metformin van causes a deficiency in which vitamin?	Vit B12
How to remember hyperthyroidism in relation to temp and weight?	Remember that thyroid and TSH are vs (Hyperthyroid will have low TSH), next Hyperthyroid High temp and low weight

Describe Addison's disease in three words?	Cortical adrenal insufficiency
Positive antithyroglobulin antibody, think?	Hashimoto's disease
What A1C level indicated DM2?	> 6.5
Statin MOA?	Inhibit HMG-CoA reductase
4 patient groups, that will benefit from statins?	1.Clinical ASCVD 2.LDL>190 3. Diabetes patients with LDL 70-189 4. LDL 70-189 and 10-year ASCVD risk score >7.5%
MC used high-intensity statins?	Atorvastatin and Rosuvastatin
MC reason to give statins at night?	Cholesterol synthesizes at night
Statins are CI in?	Pregnancy
MC side effects of statins?	Muscle pain and soreness
MC med used to increase HDL?	Niacin - Vit B3
MC adverse effect of niacin?	Flushing
Niacin CI?	Liver disease, severe gout, PUD
Buzzwords like moon face and buffalo hump, think?	Cushing's syndrome
Treatment of hyperthyroidism during pregnancy?	PTU

ENT

MC (most common) bug in bacterial sinusitis?	S. Pneumo
Strep pharyngitis should always be treated for how long?	10 days to prevent rheumatic fever
Treatment of choice for strep pharyngitis?	PCN VK
When can patients with strep return to the school?	After being on ABX for 24hr.
Which vaccine can help prevent epiglottis?	Hib
Think epiglottitis if a child presents with?	Drooling, sitting in the **sniffing tripod position** and leaning forward
3 Ds of Epiglottitis?	Dysphagia, drooling and distress
Inspiratory **stridor** think?	Epiglottitis
Epiglottitis diagnostic test?	Lateral neck x-ray showing the **Thumbprint sign**
Otitis Media (OM) treatment?	Amoxicillin 90mg/kg/day divided into 2 doses x 10 days
MC bug causing Otitis media?	S. Pneumonia
OM treatment if the patient has a PCN allergy?	Ceftriaxone, Cefdinir
What's considered recurrent OM?	3+ episodes of AOM in 6 months or 4+ in one year
Perforated TM due to infection treatment?	Amoxicillin + Ofloxacin drops

If amoxicillin fails the next step in the management of OM is?	Augmentin
MC bug causing the Otitis Externa?	Pseudomonas
MC cause of croup?	Parainfluenza virus
Barking cough, think?	Croup
Samter's triad is?	Aspirin sensitivity, nasal polyposis, and asthma
Drug of choice for treatment of pertussis?	Macrolide (Azithromycin)
Lido to bicarb ratio?	Ratio is 9:1
MC virus causing Hand-Foot-Mouth Dz?	Coxsackie A virus
Mumps is caused by which virus?	Paramyxovirus
MC complications of mumps?	**Orchitis**, pancreatitis, can cause deafness
4 years old child with a temp of 40C, Tachy, in distress, drooling with sore throat and stridor?	Epiglottitis
Epiglottitis bug?	HIB-Haemophilus influenza
ABX for epiglottitis?	Ceftriaxone to cover H flu, plus Vanco or Clinda
Croup age?	6m-3y
Small red spots in buccal mucosa with blue/white pale centers?	Koplik spots (Measles)
Measles rash lasts how many days?	7 days

Forchheimer's spots on the soft palate?	Rubella
Lymphadenopathy is associated with which viral exanthem?	Rubella/German measles
Anaphylaxis treatment?	SQ epi (1:1000), steroids, antihistamines
Kid with lip swelling no concern to him, mom said she had similar episodes when she was pregnant?	Hereditary angioedema - autosomal dominant
Weber test will localize to?	To the affected ear
Bone conduction over air conduction is seen with?	Abnormal Rinne test
MC cause of conductive hearing loss?	OM, serous otitis and cerumen impaction
MC cause of sensory hearing loss?	Noise exposure, drugs, and aging
Otitis media is MC preceded by?	URI
Treatment for recurrent or persistent OM?	Tympanostomy
If intranasal decongestants are used >5 days this can cause?	Rhinitis medicamentosa
Treatment for allergic rhinitis?	Intranasal glucocorticoids (fluticasone)
Nasal polyps can be seen in kids with?	Cystic Fibrosis
MC cause of Mastoiditis?	Prolonged or inadequately treated of Acute Otitis Media
Mastoiditis treatment?	IV ABX and myringotomy
MC location of epistaxis?	Anterior - Kiesselbach's plexus

MC cause of epistaxis in children?	Fingernails - picking their nose
What kind of epistaxis should be referred to ENT?	Posterior bleed
MC artery involved in posterior epistaxis?	Sphenopalatine artery
Centor criteria for pharyngitis is?	Fever, tender anterior cervical adenopathy, lack of cough and pharyngotonsilar exudate
Peritonsillar abscess treatment?	Immediate drainage and IV Clindamycin
Sinusitis presentation and treatment?	Congestion, yellow/green nasal discharge, cough, scratchy throat. Face feels full. Acute <4weeks. Supportive tx if <10 days if >10 give Augmentin or doxy
Acute OM always treat which patients?	< 2yo with amoxicillin
Otitis externa treatment?	Ofloxacin
The child with epiglottitis in severe distress should go to?	OR to establish a surgical airway
Steeple sign on x-ray?	Croup
MC bug causing Peritonsillar abscess?	Strep pyogenes
Deviation of the uvula on the exam, think?	Peritonsillar abscess
Muffled hot potato voice, think?	Peritonsillar abscess
MC bug that is seen with Mastitis?	S. Aureus

Peripheral vertigo symptoms are?	Acute onset dizzy N/V. Horizontal nystagmus
Peripheral vertigo test?	Dixhallpike
Central vertigo is due to?	Lesions
First-line antibiotic treatment for epiglottitis?	Intravenous ceftriaxone
Posterior cervical lymphadenopathy, think?	EBV (MONO)
Mono patients should avoid doing what?	Contact sports for 1 month
Mono test?	Heterophile antibody test
Most frequently dx in a child presenting with fever is?	OM
Strep pneumonia treatment?	Amoxicillin 500 bid 7-10 days
Whitish scaring of the eardrum is indicative of?	Tympanosclerosis
The frontal sinus is not visible on x-ray until the age?	5
A deep infection in the space between the soft palate and tonsil?	Peritonsillar abscess
Pale buggy nasal mucous?	Allergic rhinitis
MC cause of chronic cough in children older than three years old?	Asthma
Diphtheria treatment?	Antitoxin to neutralize the toxin. Erythromycin or penicillin to eliminate bacteria.

Pertussis Dx?	Clinical- cough illness > 2 weeks, PCR nasal swab
Tetanus spasm can be reduced with?	Diazepam
Tetanus treatment?	Metronidazole + tetanus immune globulin
Abrupt stopping of steroids can cause?	Acute adrenal insufficiency
Pt presents with drooling but no cough, think?	Epiglottitis
Tx for BPPV?	Epley maneuvers and meclizine
TX for mountain sickness?	Acetazolamide
The symptoms of allergic rhinitis include?	Runny nose (rhinorrhea), sneezing, nasal congestion, conjunctivitis, and itching of the ears, eyes, nose, and throat.
Atopy is what?	Hypersensitive or allergic state involving an inherited predisposition.
In the common cold, the mucosa is usually?	Red with thickened discharge, whereas with allergies the nasal mucosa appears pale and boggy or bluish.
1st line meds for allergies?	Antihistamines. The first-generation H1 antagonists
Cromolyn sodium is what?	Mast cell stabilizer. Best used for allergic rhinitis in children and pregnancy
Ménière disease is what?	Increased pressure within the semicircular canals

Ménière disease triad?	Decreased hearing, tinnitus, vertigo
Medications used to treat labyrinthitis, vestibular neuronitis, and BPV include?	Meclizine, dimenhydrinate, antiemetics, and benzodiazepines
Ménière disease treatment?	HTCZ and decrease salt
What is the treatment for croup?	Nebulized saline or nebulized racemic epinephrine for children with resting stridor.
Acute sinusitis test of choice?	CT
When do we give ABX for sinusitis?	If symptoms are present for >10 days (<7 is viral)
MC bug in chronic sinusitis?	S. Aureus
Pale boggy turbinates, think?	Allergic rhinitis
Allergic rhinitis tx?	Intranasal steroids, oral anti-histamines
Aphthous ulcers are associated with which HHV?	HHV6
Describe Aphthous ulcers	Oval painful ulcers with erythematous halos on the buccal or labial mucosa
Aphthous ulcers tx?	Topical oral steroids (triamcinolone)
Cholesteatoma is MC due to?	Chronic ET dysfunction
Cholesteatoma causes what kind of hearing loss?	Conductive hearing loss

Cholesteatoma dx?	Otoscope will show granulation tissue, Rinne test Bone > air conduction.
MC artery involved in the posterior epistaxis?	Palantine artery
What's Labyrinthitis?	Inflammation of the vestibular portion of CN 8
Labyrinthitis tx?	Meclizine
What kind of nystagmus is seen with Meniere's disease?	Horizontal
Tx for severe vertigo?	Diazepam
TX for Meniere disease?	Low sodium diet and diuretics
Treatment of choice for Nasal polyps?	Intranasal steroids
OE presentation?	Pain on the traction of the ear canal/tragus, edema, erythema
OE tx if there is a TM ruptures?	Ofloxacin
MCC (most common cause) of Parotitis?	Paramyxovirus
If pt has bilateral swollen parotids, that is indicative of?	Mumps
Complications of mumps?	Orchitis in males
Mumps are MCC of what in children?	Acute pancreatitis

Muffled hot potato voice and uvula deviation to the contralateral side, think?	Peritonsillar abscess
MCC of Peritonsillar abscess?	Strep pyogenes (GABHS)
Peritonsillar abscess dx?	CT
Peritonsillar abscess tx?	ABX + needle aspiration or I+D
MC duct involved in Sialadenitis?	Wharton's duct
Sialadenitis tx?	Hard candies, massage if that fails Lithotripsy
MC bug causing the Sialadenitis?	S. Aureus
Sialadenitis dx?	CT
Unilateral sensorineural hearing loss is?	Acoustic neuroma until proven otherwise
MC site of Tympanic membrane perforation?	MC occurs at the pars tensa
MC neurologic finding in Paget's disease?	Deafness
Acoustic neuroma traid?	Loss of hearing, tinnitus, and ataxia
MC cause of sensory-neural hearing loss?	Presbycusis
Endolymphatic hydrops, think?	Meniere's disease
Diuretic used for the treatment of Meniere's?	Acetazolamide

Mastoiditis treatment?	IV antibiotics and myringotomy are initial treatments, Mastoidectomy if persistent
Meniere's disease audiometry will show?	Low-frequency loss
Labyrinthitis presentation?	Acute severe vertigo with hearing loss and vertigo that lasts several days to 1 week
Horizontal nasal crease, think?	Allergic rhinitis
Hoarseness following URI?	Laryngitis. supportive treatment rest that voice.
Which plexus is associated with posterior nose bleed?	Woodruff plexus

Good luck on your test! You have studied hard and I'm sure you will do just fine, remember "Thousand's and thousand's of students done this before you, so can you PERIOD". **PLEASE DO ME A HUGE FAVOR AND LEAVE AN AMAZON COMMENT FOR THE BOOK. THAT HELPS ME A LOT AND LET'S OTHER STUDENTS KNOW IF YOU FOUND THIS BOOK HELPFUL. THANK YOU!!!!!!**

Obtaining patient history Template

_-Hi, my name is _____, I'm a PA student here at the _____. and I will
be taking care of you today (wash hands, shake hands, wash hands)_

Identifying data

-What do you prefer to be called?

And how old are you?

What is your gender? (If others present) _–will you introduce
everyone in the room?_

-What language do you prefer to get information in?

_-I'm going to be taking a few notes, just to make sure I don't miss
anything._

Chief Complaint (CC) Patient problem and duration

-So tell me how you're feeling today? How long?

-What do you think is going on? How long?

-What concerns do you have today? (If long list... _So we listed 5 things,
I want to address your BP and what other 2 things are most important
to talk about today? And let's schedule another visit to address..._

History of Present Illness (HPI)

-Can you tell me a little bit about this?

Onset _-Did it come on fast or slow? Gradual or sudden?_

Character -*Can you describe your symptoms?*

Location - *Where?*

Radiation -*Does it go anywhere else?*

Duration of Episodes – *how long have you had this issue?*

Frequency of Episodes –*How often does this happen?*

Factors that increase/decrease –*anything makes it better? Anything that makes it worse?*

Effect on patient -*how much is this bothering you? How is this affecting you?*

Associated symptoms -*what else is going on at that time?*

Prior similar symptoms *have you ever had something like this before?*

Treatment -*have you seen anyone for this? Or tried anything to fix this?*

Past Medical History (PMH) –*For this next section I would like to get some information about your past medical history, later we will discuss how you're feeling right now.*

Childhood/Adult Illnesses - *Can you tell me if you've had any common childhood illnesses (pause after each, if yes, how old? and any complications)? Measles? Mumps? Chicken Pox? Rheumatic Fever?*

Data Collection Template

-Have you ever had issues with your heart (cardiovascular disease)? Any history of stroke? HTN? Have you ever had lab work show you have high cholesterol (hyperlipidemia)? Any history of cancer? Diabetes? What about epilepsy? Any history of TB? Have you ever been told you have issues with your thyroid (thyroid disease)? Any history of addictions? Have you had any issues with arthritis? What about asthma? Any issues with sleeping like sleep apnea? Any history of STDs? Any other recurring diseases?

-I'm going to ask a few questions about your mental health because it's a part of your physical health – have you had any diagnosis with anxiety? Depression? -Because abuse is pretty common in our society; I've begun to ask about it routinely. Have you had any history of abuse, emotional? Physical? Sexual? Do you have a history of any eating disorders? (If yes, can you tell me a little about that? Is it an issue now?) -Have you ever sought treatment for anything I haven't mentioned? Have you had any other issues I might have missed?

Hospitalizations/Injuries/Surgeries

Allergies

-Have you ever been hospitalized? When (year)? What was the diagnosis? What about treatment? What was the outcome? -Have you had any major injuries, stuff you had to go to the hospital for? When (year)? What was the diagnosis? What about treatment? What was the outcome?

-What about any surgeries? When? What was the diagnosis? Treatment? Outcome?

-Are you allergic to anything? What happens (reaction)? When was the last time this happened? -What about any drug sensitivities? What happens? -Any environmental allergies? Any food allergies?

Before we move on to review all your medications, was there anything else about past health problems that I might have missed?

Current & Recent Medications

-It's important for your health that I know what Rx/OTC medications, herbs, and vitamins you take.

-Let's start with prescriptions? Name? Dosage? Frequency? How long have you been taking it (duration)? What is it for indication)? -Are you taking any OTC meds? Name? Dosage? Frequency? How long? What for?

-What about any herbs or vitamins? Name? Dosage?

Frequency? How long? What for? -What about any contraception?

Health Maintenance

Because I care about your overall health we want to look at your health maintenance, things like immunizations and screening tests.

Immunization Status

Have you had any immunizations for Td? -What about Tdap? -The flu vaccine? -What about Pneumovax? -Hepatitis A/B?

-What about the MMR vaccine? -HPV? (Cancer prevention) -Zoster vaccine? (Shingles given 65+) -Any other vaccines I have not

mentioned?

Screening Tests

Screening tests are important because they help us catch things before they happen, so I'm going to ask you about that.

-Have you had a PAP test? HPV test? -Have you had a mammogram? (If yes, any abnormal ones?) -Do you do breast self-exams? -What about any screening for colon cancer? -What about any tests for cholesterol? -Have you had any HIV screening? -What about any screening for prostate cancer? -Any genetic testing? -Any other screening/tests I have not mentioned?

Occupational & Environmental Exposures

Safety is a big part of overall health so I want to check in about some big safety things

-Every time you're in the car, do you wear a seat belt? -Do wear a helmet when you do any activities like ride a bike, or snowboard, rollerblade? -Do you have smoke or carbon monoxide detectors? And do they work? How often you check the batteries? -Do you have any firearms? If yes, we encourage that they are locked and secure (because there are >30k deaths in the US per year we just need to make sure that everyone is being safe. So I'm glad to hear that you're a responsible owner).

Family History (FHx)

Because many diseases run in families, it's important for me to ask about their medical history as well.

-Can you tell me if your parents are alive? How old? How is their health? (If passed away, how old when they died? From what?)

-Do you have any siblings? How old are they? How is their health? -Do you have any children? How old are they? How is their health?

-I'm going to list a few specific medical issues, let me know if anyone in your family has these. -Any trouble with the heart or blood vessels, like cardiovascular Diseases, hx of stroke? High BP, high cholesterol? -Any hx cancer? Diabetes? Epilepsy? -How about TB? Any problems with their Thyroid? Arthritis? Asthma? -Anyone in your family has any addictions? -What about any recurring diseases? -Mental health is a part of physical health, has anyone in your family suffered from depression or anxiety? -Any other things I might have missed?

Social History (SHx)

Because what people do has an impact on their health I want to get a few details about your social history.

- Can you tell me how far you went in school (education)? -What do you do for work (occupation)?

-What do you do for fun? What do you do to stay active (recreation)?

-Tell me about the foods you eat? Do you have any concerns about your diet? - Do you drink any soda/sugary drinks? -Do you drink any caffeine?

-Do you use any tobacco? If yes, what kind? How much per day? How long have you been smoking? - Tell me about your alcohol use? If yes, about how many drinks you have in a day/week?

CAGE: Have you ever thought about cutting down? Have you ever gotten annoyed when people talk to you about your drinking?

Do you ever have a drink first thing in the morning? -We've talked about alcohol and tobacco, do you use any other substances recreationally (drug use)? - Have you had a history of using any drugs you inject?

-Tell me about your home life; is there someone special in your life? Who is part of your support structure (sig. other)?

Review of Systems (ROS) *–we will do a full head to toe exam in a bit, I first want to gather some information about your general health.*

General *-Have you had any recent weight change? -What about any recent change in appetite? -Any fatigue? Or dizziness?*

Skin *-Can you tell me about any skin concerns or changes? Any itchiness (pruritus)? Or rashes?*

Eyes *-When was your last eye exam? Any changes in your vision? Do you wear any corrective lenses? Do you have any issues with double-vision (diplopia)? What blurring?*

Ears *-What about your hearing, have you noticed any hearing loss? Do you notice any ringing (tinnitus) in your ears?*

How about any ear pain? (If yes, clarify how long, which Side?)

Nose *-Do you have any sinus problems? Do you get Nosebleeds (epistaxis)?*

Mouth/Throat *-When was your last dental exam? Do you have any* dental problems? Do you wear dentures? Have you noticed any changes in your vocal quality (hoarseness)?

Neck -Do you have any pain or swelling in your neck?

Breasts -It's important for me to ask about your breast health, have you noticed any pain? Any masses? Skin changes? What about any discharge?

Cardiopulmonary -Do you ever have any chest pain? Do you ever experience your heart racing (palpitations)? Has anyone ever told you, you have a murmur? Do you ever have to stop and rest while you're walking because your legs hurt (claudication)? Have you ever passed out or felt like you're going to pass out (syncope)? Have you ever coughed up blood (hemoptysis)? Do you have any wheezing, do you notice if you make any sound when you breathe out? What about difficulty breathing or getting SOB (dyspnea)? What about if you were to lay down flat, do you have trouble breathing (orthopnea)? Do you ever wake up gasping/ coughing (PND)? Do you have any swelling (edema)? What about exercise tolerance change, like getting SOB?

Gastrointestinal -Next, I want to ask you about your GI tract, have you noticed any abdominal pain? What about heartburn? Do you ever feel like you're going to throw up (nausea)? Swallowing any vomiting? Do you ever throw up blood (hematemesis)? Do you have any trouble (dysphagia)? If yes, with liquids or solids? -I'm going to ask you some questions about your bowel movement (bowel habit change)? Anything different for you? Have you noticed any changes in the shape? Is there a change in frequency? Any issues with diarrhea? (Clinically- more than 3 BM per day) Is it painful to go to the bathroom (constipation)? Do you ever have any accidents when you lose a little bit of stool (incontinence)? Do you ever notice that your stool is dark/tarry (melena)? Have you ever noticed that your stool is bright red (hematochezia)? Do you have any rectal pain? Any bumps, redness/itching (hemorrhoids)? Any hernia?

Genitourinary

-Do you have difficulty/pain while urinating (dysuria)? -Do you feel like you have to go to the bathroom more than normal (frequency)? Do you feel like you have to go, even if you just went (urgency)? Do you feel like you have to wait extra long time to urinate (hesitancy)? ---Do you notice any discharge? How many times a night do you have to get up to urinate (nocturia)? Do you ever notice any blood in your urine (hematuria)? Do you ever have any accidents with urine (incontinence)? -Have you thought about extending your family at all? What are you doing to prevent pregnancies? (Contraception and conception planning)?

Male

-When you urinate, has that changed how much comes out (decreased stream)? Any testicular pain? Do you do self-exams? Have you noticed anything strange? -Sexual health is an important part of your overall health; do you have any concerns about skin changes/lesions, orgasm function, sex drive (sexual dysfunction)?

Female

-How many times have you been pregnant (GP gravita para)? How many pregnancies have you carried to term (GT)? How many didn't make it to term (P)? How many pregnancies have you lost (A)? How many children are living (L)? When was your last menstrual period

(LMP)? When was your last normal menstrual period (LNMP)? Any menstrual changes? Do you have any vaginal bleeding? - Sexual health is an important part of your overall health, do you have any concerns about this (sexual dysfunction)? Do you have pain during intercourse (dyspareunia)?

Sexual Habits *-I routinely ask all patients about their sexual function, when you have sex, is it with men, women, or both? -What are you doing to prevent STDs?*

Musculoskeletal *-Tell me about any joint pain? Any joint swelling? Any stiffness? Do you have any back pain? -Do you notice any difficulties with your Activities for Daily Living?*

Endocrine *-If everyone is comfortable in the room, are you ever too hot or too cold (temperature intolerance)? - Any changes with your hair, falling out, or brittle (hair changes)? Do you have excessive thirst (polydipsia)? Excessive urination (polyuria)?*

Neurologic *-Do you get headaches? Any numbness, tingling, or burning (sensory changes)? Do you ever have any shaking you can't control (tremor)? Any weakness?*

Psychiatric *-MH is part of your physical health, so I'm going to ask you about that. Do you have any issues with anxiety? What about depression? -Have you noticed any changes in your mood? Tell me about your sleep (sleep disturbances)?*

Hematologic

-Have you ever had any blood clots anywhere (DVT)? -Do you bruise

easily, without any trauma? Every time you use your gentle

toothbrush, do you notice bleeding gums? Have you had any blood

transfusions?

Now I would like to examine you.

Good luck on your test! You have studied hard and I'm sure you will do just fine, remember "Thousand's and thousand's of students done this before you, so can you PERIOD". **PLEASE DO ME A HUGE FAVOR AND LEAVE AN AMAZON COMMENT FOR THE BOOK. THAT HELPS ME A LOT AND LET'S OTHER STUDENTS KNOW IF YOU FOUND THIS BOOK HELPFUL. THANK YOU!!!!!!**

Made in United States
Orlando, FL
27 March 2025

59900911R00153